SACRED GROUND

STICKY FLOORS

JAMI AMERINE

HARVEST HOUSE PUBLISHERS
EUGENE, OREGON

Cover by Connie Gabbert Design + Illustration

Cover photos © the8monkey / Shutterstock ; MMassel / Getty

Published in association with Kirkland Media Management, L.L.C., P.O. Box 1539, Liberty, Texas 77575

Names and details have been changed in some real-life stories to protect the privacy of the individuals involved.

Sacred Ground, Sticky Floors

Copyright © 2018 Jami Amerine
Published by Harvest House Publishers
Eugene, Oregon 97408
www.harvesthousepublishers.com

ISBN 978-0-7369-7061-7 (pbk.)
ISBN 978-0-7369-7062-4 (eBook)

Library of Congress Cataloging-in-Publication Data

Names: Amerine, Jami, author.
Title: Sacred ground, sticky floors / Jami Amerine.
Description: Eugene, Oregon : Harvest House Publishers, [2018] | Includes
   bibliographical references.
Identifiers: LCCN 2018008241 (print) | LCCN 2018021488 (ebook) | ISBN
   9780736970624 (ebook) | ISBN 9780736970617 (pbk.)
Subjects: LCSH: Mothers—Religious life. | Motherhood—Religious
   aspects—Christianity.
Classification: LCC BV4529.18 (ebook) | LCC BV4529.18 .A44 2018 (print) | DDC
   248.8/431--dc23
LC record available at https://lccn.loc.gov/2018008241

Printed in the United States of America

18 19 20 21 22 23 24 25 26 / BP-SK / 10 9 8 7 6 5 4 3 2 1

To my husband, Justin—I like you.

To my children:
Maggie, for the gift of grace.
John, for making me brave.
Luke, for making me real.
Sophie, for wisdom.
Sam, for expanding my borders.
Charlie, for showing me I can.
Joy-Baby...for the joy. Pure joy.

And for every child we welcome,
whether you stay or go,
may you know the truth of Jesus Christ,
that you are of noble birth and
you were loved fearlessly
here on the sacred ground.

CONTENTS

Foreword by Katie M. Reid   7

Introduction: The Spill 11

Part 1: Relent and Reprieve

1. The Shame Game 25
2. Not Even Remotely in Control 35
3. Pretty Pictures 47
4. Greener Grass 55
5. Fear Factory 65
6. I So Proud You Is Smart 73
7. Grieftastic 81
8. Once Upon a Time… 87

Part 2: Reward and Receive

9. Night Night 101
10. Secret Sauce 113
11. A Shoulder to Blow My Nose On 125
12. Shoulda, Coulda, Woulda 131
13. Catch and Release 143
14. Philosophies, Legalities, and Singing Raccoons 155
15. Simply Loving Well 165
16. She Seems Familiar 173
17. Seeds and Weeds 185

Epilogue 193

Afterword by Luke Amerine 199

More from Jami Amerine 201

Notes 215

FOREWORD

I was a know-it-all mom until that inaugural night in the hospital with my first child. "I would never" statements quickly became fallacies as I agreed—from the foggy haze of sleep deprivation—my infant could have formula and a pacifier. Of course, there is nothing wrong with this, but try telling that to an overly ambitious first-time mama. I was shocked when my well-calculated plan was challenged by an eight-pound, three-ounce little darling.

Motherhood continued to unravel my tightly wound self with all its bumps, twists, and surprises. I have five really great kids (a toddler, a kindergartner, two tweens, and a teen), but they are far from angelic and definitely strong-willed (just like their mom). I used to think that if I just tried harder, my kids would act better. But the harder I tried, the more discouraged I felt.

These glorious humans have a mind of their own, which doesn't often line up with my unrealistic, lofty ideals. When I try to parent from a place of perfection, I set us all up for frustration. Yet I don't want to throw in the towel either, because raising these children is a noble calling, and they have amazing things to offer the world. For instance, one of them helped initiate a campaign to fund a well for a needy community overseas. Another child holds doors open for others without prompting. And one son begged me to give his allowance to a homeless man.

It can be tempting to measure our worth by the exemplary behavior of our offspring, or to discount our worth because of their foolish choices. Yet Jami invites us to parent from a different perspective. One that is steeped in hope and not puffed up by accolades or sabotaged by sticky circumstances.

Sacred Ground, Sticky Floors contains a refreshing dose of hilarity mixed with heart-wrenching moments and topped with guilt-lifting revelations.

Jami writes from a place of raising man-babies and a runaway bride, parenting a prodigy, fostering littles, and carting around vandals. She has launched some of her kids, wants to drop-kick a couple, and loves them all fiercely. Jami no longer parents from a place of panic.

And we don't have to either. We don't have to wring our hands, think through every worst-case scenario, or hide the fact that our children are far from perfect. Our lack of having it together is cause for Jesus to be enough for us (parents and offspring alike).

Jami wisely offers, "Yes, I can comfort and love and nurture. But if I fix everything for everyone, why do they need Jesus? If I'm meeting every single tear or whimper with warm chocolate chip cookies and physical and spiritual Band-Aids, when will they fall into the arms of their Jesus?"

Do we want the best for our kids? Of course. But we can't force them into pure belief or give them a willing heart to receive His goodness. That's above our pay grade. The best thing we can do is receive the strength and grace of our Heavenly Father and walk out our birthright as His daughters. As our kids watch us do that, I believe they will be forever changed.

Jami gently guides us to the heart of non-frantic parenting. Come on in, pardon the sticky, and discover how to parent from a place of peace.

—**Katie M. Reid**
author of *Made Like Martha*
(from a loud room in her home,
with children throwing things)

Introduction

THE SPILL

All of us who have had that veil removed can see
and reflect the glory of the Lord. And the Lord—
who is the Spirit—makes us more and more like
him as we are changed into his glorious image.

2 CORINTHIANS 3:18

He arrived by state transport in a worn and tattered car seat. It was the Thursday evening before a long holiday weekend when the '90s silver Toyota Corolla pulled up in front of our Texas home. The evening was still slightly warm, and the sky was exploding with all the colors of the setting sun. On this cul-de-sac, a symphony of tragedy and triumph played out as a battered baby boy arrived safely at his new home.

My family, all seven of us, stood on the front porch and watched as the plump woman from the state tugged at the car seat, with the mystery boy strapped inside, and finally finagled it out of the impossibly tiny back seat. My eldest daughter, Maggie, put both hands over her eyes and, under her breath, gasped, "Please be careful."

The state representative, aware of the spectacle in which she was center stage, waved and offered assurances. "Got it! Sorry, I'm not used to these big car seats!" My husband, Justin, walked over to help. She halted him with one hand and said, "You can take my briefcase." The boy was still her ward and responsibility. He did not yet belong to our arms, our home, our hearts.

As the woman lugged the precious cargo into the house, my husband followed her. His looks spoke volumes, morphing from expressions of disgust to concern and then on to exasperation. Finally, the woman placed the carrier with the injured baby on the formal dining room table, and we tried to concentrate on the overwhelming process of signing documents and listening to instructions.

Our four older children stood and stared, in both love and heartache, at the small creature peacefully sleeping in the shabby car seat. Sam, our three-year-old, kept pointing at the baby, giggling and saying, "Bebe! Bebe! Sam holds da bebe!"

After affixing 500 signatures to at least 4,000 documents, we took the state representative on a walk-through of our home. We gave a thorough explanation of the mechanics of our fire extinguisher; provided copies of our evacuation plan in case Russia invaded; showed her where we kept our prescriptions, cleaning products, and unmentionables; and finally waved goodbye.

We were now a family of eight.

Welcome to the Family

Battered. Broken. Bruised. A little cherub with pink cheeks and doe eyes. Although "Charlie" was barely four months old, a tiny cast enveloped his wee limb. He smelled of an unknown origin and the hospital. He cooed, just a bit, and his voice was notably raspy. (At the time, we believed it was from crying, but we've since realized it's just part of his unique "Charlie charm.") I had spent the two days prior at the hospital with the boy; I prayed he would remember me and not be afraid or confused. He opened his eyes and smiled at me. For that moment, my heart skipped a beat, and I could barely breathe. We all stood over him. We were speechless.

We had taken the classes. Talked about the possibilities and readily agreed, "Sure we can!" But now, here he was. Fully human, fully damaged, fully in need. The full reality of him was overwhelming.

I wanted to make it all better. I wanted justice for those broken limbs. I wanted healing. I wanted him to know Jesus. I wanted his story to be different, and yet I wanted to know his story. How does this happen? How could anyone hurt an *infant*?

Finally, one of the kids broke the silence and said, "His head is *enormous*!" and we all burst into laughter and tears.

"Welcome to the family, kid!" said another. "Let the razzing begin!"

We spent the rest of the night gently passing him around, giving him a sponge bath, feeding him, and figuring out how to change his diapers without disturbing his wounded limbs. We made bottles, washed his tiny clothes, and joyfully served the least of these as a family.

Down Came the Cider

The next days were nothing short of exhausting. Charlie was in pain, and unless I held him, swaddled, he was despondent. I slept in a chair in the corner of our master suite with him upright on my chest to keep the pressure off his broken frame.

After a sleepless Saturday night, I needed to talk to someone. On Sunday morning, I sent a text to a precious friend, a seasoned foster mom who says wise and beautiful things. I filled her in on the events of the last few days and told her I was drained and needed to hear a friendly word.

I hit *send* and waited. She would say something fabulous, and I would be energized for the day. My phone buzzed, and I grabbed it, impatient to see what dear jewels of love and affirmation she would send. I read her words with an unquenchable eagerness:

"What a precious little lamb! You and your family are blessed to be at his service. I encourage you to keep a journal of this special time with this baby boy. You are on sacred ground."

What?

I started to type "LOL" but then worried she wasn't kidding. "Sacred ground"? I didn't see any burning bushes around. I had no poignant response, so I just typed, "Thanks," and proceeded to drudge on with my day.

On Monday afternoon, Justin and the older kids were running errands. I was enjoying the rare peace of having fewer humans in the house. Three-year-old Sam took a nice long nap while I worked on bills. I had Charlie swaddled to my body with some mysterious contraption that had been invented since the last time I had babies. As long as my movements were slow, he was comfortable, and more than anything I wanted him not to hurt. I continued to work, feet up on the chair across from me, a Wonder Woman mug to my right holding steaming coffee. I marveled at my abilities.

A bit later, Sam wandered into the kitchen with sleep-mussed hair, his face drowsy. I greeted him. "Hey, Sam-I-am! Did you have a good nap?"

He nodded, yawned, and said, "Mommy, I want some juice."

I nodded absentmindedly. "Just let me finish filling out this form, and I'll get you some."

Sam climbed onto a stool next to the kitchen island, where an enormous jug of apple cider from Costco was sitting. "Sam do it!" he said.

"No, Sam! Mommy will get you juice," I said. "Just a second!" The jug was nearly full, and it was roughly the same size as Sam. From where I sat I could tell it had been opened; someone hadn't screwed on the cap securely.

Sam pulled his Thomas the Tank Engine cup closer to the juice. "It's *my* turn, Mommy."

Carefully, so as not to hurt the baby, I pulled my legs down from the chair and stepped barefoot onto the cold tile. As the blood returned to my legs, I realized both my feet were asleep. "No. No. No. Sam, Mommy will do it!" My feet were tingling, and the tension from holding Charlie flared in my back. The instinct to stop him was slowed by the desire not to cause myself or the baby any pain. "Sam, *stop!*"

Sam ignored me.

The little boy was no match for the bargain barrel of cider. He tilted it, and it fell to its side, rolled off the island, and exploded. The juice splashed six feet straight up, spraying Sam, me, the baby, the cabinets, and the ceiling. I stood speechless.

"Sorry, Mommy."

I could barely hear Sam because, in my mind, I was loudly and clearly explaining to him why he must wait for Mommy to help pour his juice. I could hear myself telling him he needed to go to time-out for disobeying me. In reality, only a whimper escaped my lips. Tears stung my eyes. *Wait. I am a seasoned, professional mommy. Am I crying? Literally* crying *over a spilled drink?* I could feel the cider river expanding beneath me. *Do we have flood insurance?* The whimper turned to sobs. Heaving sobs.

The human being strapped to my body began to stir. I heard Sam's muffled apologies, and I could hear the garage door open. I still didn't move. I felt the cider being absorbed into the cuffs of my jeans. Through my tears, I saw the rest of the family appear in the kitchen doorway.

Sam said, "Look, guys! Mommy is crying really hard."

"What *happened?*" asked my husband.

Through my childish sobs, I wept, "Oh, Justin...we're going to have to move."

My friend's words, "You are on sacred ground," rattled around in my head for days after "The Spill." They were whispered into my ear at the oddest of times. Once while giving Sam a bath, another time while I was sautéing onions, and again while changing a poopy diaper. On a couple of occasions, I had thought of texting my friend and flat out asking her what she could have possibly meant…but I was afraid I would sound dumb. So I let it go.

Still, the whisper returned.

Surrender on Sacred Ground

About two weeks after "The Spill," I relaxed my exhausted body in the semi-comfy recliner, in our master suite where I continued to spend my nights with Charlie. My head fell back, and I drifted off to sleep. My leopard-print-slippered feet curled under me. The baby lay on my chest in the only position where he could find comfort and rest. And I heard the whisper again: *You are on sacred ground.*

I opened my eyes to look around the room. This time, the words had been nearly audible. Moonlight crept under the blinds. I kicked off a slipper and set my foot on the carpet. The ball of my foot discovered a sticky spot…*apple juice.* From the office-turned-nursery off our master bedroom, I heard Sam making car noises in his bed. Justin rolled to his side and began to snore.

You are on sacred ground.

I could hear the four older children in the kitchen. Good grief, they were eating. *Again.* The smell of popcorn and bacon, of all things, wafted under the bedroom door. Suddenly, there was a loud but familiar crash. The clock in the kitchen had fallen off the wall. *Again.* The crash was followed by snorts of laughter, the thud of punches, and the girls' whisper-yells of "Guys! Shhhhh!"

I snatched my phone off the arm of the chair and fired off a group text to the kids: "You will wake the babies and your father!

Be quiet and clean up your mess!" Sophie, our youngest daughter, texted me back: "OK! LOL! SORRY! ILYSM."

I stared at the last part of Sophie's text. What? Oh! I knew that one. I texted her back: *I love you so much too. Night.* The kitchen exploded with laughter. *Again.* They think it's funny when I figure out the texting lingo.

I laid my head back, closed my eyes, and began a mental grocery list. I would have to buy more bacon. Milk, bread, avocados, and something nice to put in Justin's lunch, just to spice things up… maybe some of his favorite pickles.

You are on sacred ground.

The baby stirred on my chest. His movements caused him to whimper. I whispered, "Jesus, grant this boy comfort and rest."

In that moment, I felt the warmth of God's presence. He doesn't leave. He is with me. With us. I dared not move or blink out of fear that I would either disturb the little guy or lose the strong sense of Jesus. How I wish my heart always felt this peace.

The child sighed. I yawned and felt myself starting to drift off once more. Before I reached a state of blissful sleep, the words arose again.

You are on sacred ground.

As I felt the little one's body melt into mine, I didn't pause to question my friend's insight. I surrendered to it.

Yes. I am on sacred ground.

Because God Is There

I admit that before my friend sent her text, it never occurred to me that this life, this home, could be sacred ground. But now, "You are on sacred ground" has become a mantra of sorts for me. A daily reminder to behold what God is doing. (So far, I've been accused only once of being sacrilegious by claiming my home is sacred ground.)

I'm sure the words "sacred ground" conjure up some images for you and, most likely, they aren't visions of where you are standing right now. If, like me, you've stepped on a Lego while barefoot, it can be difficult to wrap your mind around the divine qualities of the path beneath your feet.

But when we know what to look for, everything changes.

I propose that the place where you stand now, the place where you care for and lead those you love, is sacred ground.

When I was growing up, we had a large white family Bible made of fake leather, with big gold letters on the front: HOLY BIBLE. It was on the coffee table for as long as I can remember. I liked to look at the pictures. Perhaps because I'm dyslexic, I'm very visual. So I spent hours looking at pictures of famous biblical paintings in that huge King James edition. Three specific works of art spoke most to my young heart and mind.

The first was of Jesus on the cross with Mary at His feet. The sky was painted this icky brown color, and Jesus, in spite of His horrific injuries, was clean, with only little trickles of blood on His hands and feet. The crown of thorns was carefully set on His brow, not pressed into his flesh like I would see later in other paintings and depictions. His mother was clinging to the foot of the cross and had a single tear on her cheek.

The second picture was a black-and-white image of Daniel in the lion's den. I am sure you've probably seen this one. In it, Daniel peacefully stands to gaze at the sky from his would-be tomb. His back is to many lions. The lions are just as tranquil as Daniel, unprovoked to devour the prophet because he belongs to the Master of all, the living God.

The third painting was of Moses. In it, he is sitting on a rock, removing his sandals. In front of him is a bush, and it is on fire. Of the hundreds of times I looked at these pictures during my childhood, this one made me the most curious. Why was it important?

Yes, a bush caught fire and a voice came out of it, but in the scope of parted seas, plagues, talking serpents, tame lions, virgin births, and the Son of Man being raised from the dead, it was hardly epic. Certainly, the moment did have one unique element: God saying, "Take off your shoes, Moses. You are on sacred ground." Why that spot? Is it still sacred now, or was it only sacred when God was there?

Forty-five years later, I have my answer. It was sacred because God was there. There in the mountains, a man who was guiding sheep—a caretaker, but not yet a leader—went hiking through the rocky terrain. The Lord called out to him in the place where Moses could hear and receive a message. In this location where they talked, Moses *was* on sacred ground.

I realize now that each of the scenes etched into my memory were images of sacred ground. Mary, kneeling at the foot of her son's cross; Daniel, surrounded by the enemy, yet safe in the unseen protection of the Lord; Moses, called to something greater by a talking shrub that was on fire—all *sacred ground.*

Your home is holy too. The living God wanders your halls, searches your heart, and dwells among your family. The place where your family comes to know that you love and lean on Jesus Christ to get you through sleepless nights, apple-juice spills, and all the trials of motherhood and life is sacred ground.

I am the mother of children by birth, adoption, and foster-love. There is no end to the adjectives that describe these children, these individual pieces of my soul: military, teen, tween, birth, foster, adoptive, college-aged, preschool-aged, infant, grade-school-aged, high-school-aged, homeschooled, married, engaged, handcuffed, shipped off, reformed, searching, found, broken, bound, set free.

Even when you don't keep adding kids to your family portraits, the children you do have are adding to that list of descriptions, needs, stages, and phases.

Pictures on the wall surround me; pictures of my babies. Pictures of smiles, laughter, joy. Pictures that depict my heart. I love all my children. They are wholly a part of me, and wholly apart from me. And they are a part of my 23-year journey to freedom through belief in a good God.

I have not been the perfect mother. My background is in education. My learning philosophy is "Success breeds success." And I fail regularly. I don't have all the answers to the struggles of parenting, and I'm not sure this is the perfect time to write this message—shouldn't I wait until I'm more whole, until I'm further along in this journey? But imperfect timing is sometimes the perfect time to share with each other from the broken places and empty spaces.

So here I am.

Like the photos that surround me now, my offerings in this book are scenes, glimpses of different times and moments that have captured my heart, reshaped my faith, and mended broken places. They don't follow the order of calendars, but instead follow the path of a mama's memories and heart lessons. I share from that journey as you and I look more closely at what it is to stumble and get up again under the covering of grace. In this place, I have not loved perfectly but, friend, I have loved well, and I have *been* loved most perfectly.

I look back at where I came from and how I got to this place of adult children, toddlers, and temporary foster-loves, and while I still haven't completely grasped who God is, I know there is no way He is anything like the old me.

The calamity that is my life doesn't influence the power of Yahweh. He is privy to the devil's old tricks.

Your life's voice is born of your life's journey. God's voice in your life is born of the Word, and it *always* applies to your journey.

He will provide and comfort. It is in this place——your life, your home—that His Word is your truth and breath. He will be unmistakably present in those moments. His presence will become more and more evident, the sound of His voice clearer. Be still. Let Him be God. Let Him wander your halls, search your heart, and dwell among your family. He will walk through apple juice and step over the piles of laundry because His grace is everlasting. A simple *yes* is all He waits for.

The thing I am certain of is that God is real, He is for us, and He is totally invested in you and your family here on the sacred ground—sacred ground with very sticky floors.

Part 1

RELENT AND REPRIEVE

God doesn't want something from us;
He simply wants us.

GERALD L. SITTSER[1]

The place where
we and our
children are
hurting, in trouble,
or in need is the
very place He looks
on and comforts
as Father.

Chapter 1

THE SHAME GAME

I will forgive their wickedness,
and I will never again remember their sins.

HEBREWS 8:12

The moment arrives. A child is placed in your arms. And boy or girl, newborn infant or adopted toddler, you are officially guaranteed one very specific emotion from this day forward.

Guilt.

Congratulations.

If there is a more perfect word to be associated with motherhood, I have not uncovered it. Believe me, I've looked. The magnitude of mother guilt is like nothing any other human can experience.

Now, God sees all that guilt, and He stays. It is healing (and free therapy) to confess that we are far from perfect, and yet Jesus still dwells in us. He is constant—a devout fan—and nothing we can say or do would sway His desire to abide in His people.

With that said, allow me to shoot from my mama hip, speak my truth, lower the bar, level the parenting playing field, or whatever this whopper of a confession does. Here it goes:

I smoked when I was pregnant with my first baby.

Told ya. Whopper.

And that is merely the beginning of my bad parenting. I wasn't trying to get pregnant, so I didn't know I was pregnant at the time. But still…images of myself as Marlboro Mama haunt me.

As soon as I found out I was pregnant, I labored to kick the smelly and unhealthy habit. However, I loved to smoke. It kept me skinny and calmed me down. And back then, I was prone to try anything and everything that might help me overcome the mental terror known as "being Jami." So the attraction of this habit was not so simple to turn off. It didn't feel like an easy, obvious trade initially…my stinky cigarettes in exchange for a human to feed, burp, and diaper.

I started off feeling bad. The mother lode of guilt begins to accumulate, for some of us, at our child's conception.

From the moment I found out I was pregnant, I started believing the lie that I was going to be a terrible mother. Hating on myself was my specialty—my premium ability. And from that place of self-destruction, both mental and physical, I created a god who hated me just as much. This god was perpetually disgusted with me, my diet, my budget, my wardrobe, and the car I drove. The voice of truth that said I was God's beloved daughter was continually drowned out by the voice of defeat and condemnation, which interestingly enough sounded a lot like my own voice. My full-time job, aside from working as a receptionist at a dentist's office, attending college full time, and being an exhausted pregnant newlywed, was to hate everything about myself—and believe God did too.

But I puffed on my Marlboros and didn't talk about it. Instead, in our little pink stucco rental home on the corner of Oak Street, I played house. My husband, Justin, was beside himself with the idea of fatherhood. In our minds, our first child was a boy, and we called him "Baby Jake." We decided not to find out the sex of our baby with a sonogram because we felt certain we knew who Jake was, and we thought it was more fun not to know for sure until the delivery.

I practiced mothering on Justin. I made elaborate meals and budgeted to the penny. I was organized and efficient. I worked tirelessly to perfection and marveled at the idea of motherhood. Jake and I were already a team.

All the while, everyone in my life insisted they knew I was going to have a girl. They pressured me to pick a girl name. My mom and my mother-in-law told me about detailed dreams they had of a brown-eyed girl.

I secretly hoped they were wrong. The aspect of pregnancy that was most confusing to me was that I could be carrying a human being inside of my body and not know something, *anything*, about that human. I pictured a blond-haired, green-eyed little boy. I bought tiny boots and Wranglers and imagined Justin and Jake on the tractor out at our family ranch. But when I shared these images with anyone, including one of my best friends, the visions were met with a sigh, followed by, "I just know you are having a girl."

I daydreamed about Jake. I talked to him. Justin and I had fun looking at magazines and making plans to move to a different house with a yard and trees for our son.

Pregnancy wasn't all bliss. I had strangers touching my belly. Seriously, what is that about? Once while checking out at a grocery store, an old man walked up and just started rubbing my stomach, and I began to cry. He said, "Oh little mama, those pregnancy hormones will get you every time."

I grabbed my bags, bolted to my car, and heaved sobs as I drove. Hormones had nothing to do with losing every inch of bodily territory. Not only was I sharing my insides with a very active baby who made me wet my pants and would stretch and push so hard you could see perfect imprints of tiny feet just under my rib cage, but the outside of my body was free rein too?

I was weepy, sleepy, grumpy, and exasperated. However, for the first time in my life, I had a friend, a constant companion. Jake was with me, and no matter what anyone said, I fully believed I knew my son. I was utterly ecstatic with the idea of this baby boy.

Then came Maggie.

Swapping Lies for Love

"It's a girl!"

What? I was bewildered. Stunned.

In the hours and days that followed the birth of my daughter, people would proudly say, "I knew it was a girl!" or "I told you so!" They felt confirmed and wise. I felt as if I had lost someone I knew… someone who hadn't existed. Jake.

Of course, I adore Maggie. Of course, God knew what He was doing and why. But the fact is, I was confused and faced with a season of loss when she was born. And those emotions produced another passion that would become a trademark of my parenting journey: guilt, guilt, guilt.

I started that journey while Maggie was in utero as I puffed on a cigarette. I walked that journey for years, heaping guilt on myself for everything that hurt my children. *This is just what mothering is,* I thought, *self-condemnation and mental anguish over things completely out of my control.* I was most excellent at accepting condemnation and brutalizing myself to the umpteenth degree.

I know it sounds silly—feeling guilty for not knowing my child's gender before her birth. But I felt unworthy to be her mother because I hadn't recognized her for who she was. And in my unworthiness, I succumbed to every interference and let everyone else be what she needed.

My mom liked the name Maggie. My mother-in-law loved Mary. Justin loved Margaret. And so Jake became Mary Margaret, Maggie for short. I called her Magpie, and she looked at me with wisdom and genuine concern, as if to ask, "You have no idea what you're doing, do you?"

Loser

Alone the first night in that hospital room, a young mother nursed her newborn baby as I bottle-fed mine. "Loser" was branded on my engorged breasts that Maggie was unable to latch on to. *I can't even do this simple thing. I can't even feed my child.*

"What's your baby's name?" the other mother asked.

Jake stuck in my throat—and then the name I had really loved for a little girl, Piper Louise, almost spilled from my lips. But when it came time to name the girl in my arms, I hadn't had the confidence to overcome the opinions of those who "knew her" better than I.

"Mary Margaret, Maggie for short."

"Oh. That's weird."

Yes, I thought. *It is weird because I was supposed to give birth to Jake.*

"What's your baby's name?" I eagerly moved the focus off myself.

"Alaska Dawn! Like the morning sun. In Alaska."

I was the weird one? In that room with the woman who gave birth to a daughter in Texas in the afternoon and came up with the name Alaska Dawn? From that moment on, I took pride in Maggie's old-fashioned, classic name. Mary Margaret was strong, and it was biblical. Maybe I had done one thing right in keeping my mouth shut about naming her. No, I didn't know her or what I was doing, but she was healthy and beautiful.

Surely the rest of the mystery of motherhood wouldn't be as confusing or gut wrenching as pregnancy and childbirth.

(In hindsight, Shirley might have been a good name.)

Surely instinct would set in, and I would know what I was doing.

Surely I wouldn't always be this overwhelmed or my body this mushy.

This, too, was not accurate: I continue to be mystified, and my abs are still a hot mess.

Believing the Snake

With Maggie, we followed all the rules. All of them. Just as I tried to live out my faith for the legalistic god I imagined, I lived out my parenting the same way. And just as the fruit of that kind of faith was fear, the fruit of this kind of parenting was guilt, depression, and more loads of worry than even the ridiculous piles of diaper laundry.

At one point I was paranoid I had postpartum depression, without manifesting a single sign of it. I read one sign of PPD was having thoughts of hurting your baby, putting her in the oven, or dropping her off a tall building. I had no intention of doing any of those things, but I wondered if I could be caught off guard by thoughts I wasn't having and accidentally put Maggie in the oven or throw her off a building. It was exhausting, to say the least. When no one was looking, I would apologize to Maggie for being such an awful mother.

I have no proof, but I am 99 percent sure she would have nodded in agreement.

Maggie outpaced us before her second birthday. Her first sentence was, "Unfortunately, the curriculum is insufficient for my level of intelligence." At the time, we thought it was hilarious. Our laughter would come back to bite us violently in the proverbial, metaphorical, and literal sense (Maggie was a biter).

I watched other mothers with their babies and was convinced that the difference between their relationships with their Haydens, Haleys, and Ashtons and my relationship with Maggie was that my daughter was better than me. Also, she deserved better than me.

I'm certain now that these kinds of pressures, lies, and comparisons are the handiwork of the enemy. His goal is to separate us from our identity and make us believe that we are doing the most natural

The place where
you stand now,
the place where
you care for
and lead those
you love, is
sacred ground.

Chapter 2

NOT EVEN REMOTELY IN CONTROL

*Whatever is good and perfect is a gift
coming down to us from God our Father,
who created all the lights in the heavens. He never
changes or casts a shifting shadow.*

JAMES 1:17

I n a state of extreme pregnancy, I finished my master's orals at 2:30 one April afternoon in 1998. Maggie, then almost three, sat in the adjunct professor's office next door, in the education department of Hardin-Simmons University. My daughter, the perfect toddler specimen, had sat through many a lecture, sipping chicken alphabet soup out of a Blue's Clues thermos while coloring with fat crayons in a Dora the Explorer coloring book.

I leaked amniotic fluid and awesomeness as I received my congratulatory praises. I grabbed Maggie and drove home to prepare for the labor and delivery of our second baby—an event which occurred early the next morning. Once again, we had declined to know the sex of our baby during the pregnancy. Once again, my epidural only worked from my knees down.

Our baby's heartbeat was faint, and my blood pressure continued to drop. As I slipped in and out of consciousness, I saw images of frantic nurses, a distraught Justin, and, at two different points, my ob-gyn sitting next to my bed, praying.

Low blood pressure has a tranquil effect. I was completely at peace in the face of my impending death. I wasn't sad or stressed. I remember thinking how handsome Justin was and how I hoped he'd marry some cute little thing who would be a better mother to Maggie than I ever was.

I drifted off again and dreamed of a blond-haired, green-eyed boy. And then I heard someone yelling, "It's a boy! Hello, John!" I opened my eyes and saw little feet and a round tummy.

I was handed a tiny blue bundle.

I knew this boy. My father's face, my grandfather's hands, Justin's feet. John was a welcome and familiar sight.

He was tiny—a pound and a half smaller than Maggie had been at birth. The little boy followed in his sister's disdain for breastfeeding. He'd turn his head and cry, altogether refusing to nurse. He also failed his hearing test, and we were sent home with information about how often to return for more hearing testing until he passed. We took this seriously because studies showed a higher incidence of sudden infant death syndrome (SIDS) in babies who failed their hearing tests.

By John's four-month checkup, he was still failing his hearing test. One time, the shelf in our kitchen that held all our pots and pans crashed to the floor. The noise so startled and upset Maggie that it took an hour to calm her down.

John never flinched.

John slept like a champ. He would sleep 12 hours at a stretch. He was the easiest baby, which might explain why I was pregnant again in what some would consider an inappropriate amount of time. By John's first birthday, I was back in maternity clothes.

Of all the things I knew for sure, and in spite of what our days would look like with a hearing-impaired child, we were delighted with our family life. We lived in a little white house with red trim and a red front door. We grilled burgers and pushed strollers and watched Sesame Street. We were pretty sure that my current pregnancy would be my last, and that a family of five would be just right.

The Saturday night after John's first birthday party, we tucked in Maggie and John and climbed into bed with smiles on our faces and hearts full.

We awakened to a nightmare. I was soaked in blood.

We called my mother-in-law, asked her to watch Maggie and John, and went to the emergency room. There, I was told I had miscarried and to return to my ob-gyn's office on Monday for a D&C. We were crushed.

"At least it was early," friends said. "When will you try again?"

Try again? I didn't trip and fall at the finish line. This was our baby. Our baby died. I am still slain by the public's inability to recognize the depths of loss associated with miscarriage. If you are among those who have faced this loss, you know that yours is a private and enormous pain. Grieve on, but do not grieve without hope.

On Monday morning we arrived at my ob-gyn's office. The doctor insisted on an ultrasound before admitting me for a D&C procedure. One side of my uterus showed tissue loss, and on the other side clung a little peanut of a baby, heartbeat and all.

I spent the next five months in bed, John sleeping nearby, Maggie coloring like she was in grad school. We were happy about our remaining baby, and we had every right to grieve the twin who waits for us in the arms of Jesus.

The mysteries of birth, life, and death are unique for a mom who must face them when least expected. These are the most personal and organic of passages.

Let There Be Luke

In October 1999, it was time for me to give birth to the child who had lost his twin months before. I felt like I had held my breath each day of that pregnancy. I was so afraid I might lose this already greatly loved child.

So certain was I that Luke Henry was Luke Henry, it wasn't until I started pushing that I told Justin we needed to pick a girl name, just in case. But moments later, Luke arrived—with a broken collarbone. His umbilical cord was wrapped partially around his neck and shoulder. When he had moved through the birth canal, the pressure had cracked his clavicle. But he was alive. We now had three of our dear Originals. Sophie, the fourth, would arrive a few years later.

If Maggie and John were easy, Luke was impossible. He was the saddest and most beautiful baby I had ever seen. His huge green eyes and enormous dimples would save his life on more than one occasion. I can't know for sure what he lost when I miscarried his twin, but Luke was sad. He was impossible to console. If Luke was awake, he was crying. He was miserable, and we were at a loss.

The first six months were a blur. The next six months offered some relief. The year after his first birthday, Luke would fluctuate between wandering through the house weeping, as if he were looking for someone, and being an absolute cuddle-bug sweetheart. We believed we were crossing into a season of peace.

And then he turned two.

Perfect Plans, Imperfect People

When Maggie was little, we had a crazed cat named Mrs. Nezbitt that we inherited from a neighbor. Mrs. Nezbitt was smelly. She liked to roll in the mud. She was a strange beast who ate tomatoes, stole pencils, and chewed up matches.

On one occasion, my grandparents had come to visit us from Utah. My Grandma Mickey, a self-proclaimed cat whisperer, noticed how icky Mrs. Nezbitt was. She informed Maggie that she had a special secret trick for bathing cats.

Grandma Mickey explained that if you put a cat in a pillowcase and gently tied the case closed at the cat's neck with a ribbon or piece of yarn, you could then scrub the cat's body through the pillowcase without getting scratched. Maggie inverted the instructions. She put the cat's head in a pillowcase and gently tied the case closed at her neck.

Just because Mrs. Nezbitt couldn't see what was happening didn't make it any less traumatic. The wet cat with a pillowcase over its head came flying down the stairs, howling and scratching. Maggie also came flying down the stairs, right behind the enraged feline—soaked to the bone, bleeding and sobbing.

Grandma Mickey was horrified. Maggie bawled, "That special secret trick for cat washing wasn't special at *all*!" It was a good plan, of course, but even perfect plans can fail to take imperfect people into account.

Me? I like my plans. When I'm exhausted—which is all the time—I like having a formula to fall back on and to give me at least the illusion of control. Plans and formulas tell me that if I do X, Y will follow. I had earned a master's degree in human development; one would assume I had an inkling of the perfect way to rear children. If I were to follow Dobson's rules for raising up boys, Spock's rules for weaning babies, and the advice of whichever parenting guru came along next, then only good things would happen to my children. Right?

Maybe you've been parenting long enough to see that sometimes X is followed by Z.

Now, I don't believe there is one formula we need to know to save a struggling child or guide a prodigy. The key is usually found in the kids themselves—what they need, and who God created them to be. Still, we parents crave control. We love our plans. We seek answers. We want to have a solution, and we want to appear wise and informed.

In my experience, as long as the detailed home, religiosities, and life management schedule was being followed, I deemed myself well and peaceful. But with toddler Luke, the imperfect threatened to overwhelm me.

If/Then Jesus

With Luke, the special secret tricks weren't working. I was doing all the good stuff, but only bad stuff resulted.

As in parenting, so in faith. I believed in a consequential God. In all fairness, my entire life is based on the consequential.

If I put the baby to bed too early, *then* I will have to get up too early.

If the toddlers take a nap in the car, *then* I will bust free from the confines of my Weight Watchers points and eat pie and Cheez-Its.

If I don't put the laundry away as soon as it is folded, *then* it will sit on the table until Sunday lunch.

If the laundry is still on the table for Sunday lunch, *then* it will get dumped in the laundry basket and be rewashed and refolded and not put away again.

If I eat that piece of pie, *then* I will give up all hope and lose another week of healthy eating and just vow to start over on Monday—and *then* I will follow up the pie with Cheez-Its.

If I don't step onto the elliptical right now, *then* I will meet with a new level of self-loathing that will encourage the consumption of more pie and Cheez-Its.

If I sit down to watch TV with the toddlers, *then* I will lose brain cells and portions of my life I can never regain.

If the preschool teacher calls to tell me the children are vomiting, *then* I will unleash the hounds and be banned from Mother's Day Out.

If I don't cook, *then* we will have to have Cheez-Its for dinner for the third time this week.

If we have Cheez-Its for dinner again this week, *then* Justin will probably want a divorce.

If Justin and I get a divorce, *then* I will give him full custody of the kids.

If Justin gets full custody of the children, *then* I will probably just have Cheez-Its for dinner for the rest of my life—and pie for breakfast and lunch.

Steeped in an if/then lifestyle, it is hard for me to fathom a God unchanged by my actions.

In his book *God without Religion,* Dr. Andrew Farley reminds us that "God is *not* in a swivel chair, rotating his face away when we sin. Because of the cross, his face is always toward us."[1] This image of a "swivel-chair Jesus" resonated with my long-held understanding of a Lord of consequence rather than of mercy. For years I envisioned a Jesus who turned His back on me when He was displeased and spun around to face me only when I was good. What an exhausting way to believe. What an exhausting way to live.

Maybe you're exhausted by these beliefs too. Have you ever had these thoughts run through your mind?

If I get up and have my quiet time, *then* Jesus will bless me.

If I pray really hard, *then* Jesus will hear me.

If I fast, *then* God will have mercy on me.

If we don't go to church, *then* God will be furious.

If we go to church, *then* God will sanctify us.

If I continue to mess up, *then* I might get sick, or one of my children will suffer.

But no matter how good our plans and intentions, our imperfections get in the way. Our sin separates us from the living God. So

Jesus, who was and is without sin, sacrificed Himself for us. If the law had worked, then we wouldn't have needed a Savior.

The realization that Jesus sees me as blameless and whole in spite of my sin is beyond the scope of my brain. Still, these are the if/then statements I believe I need to remember:

If Jesus was the perfect sacrifice, *then* I must believe His blood worked.

If I believe, *then* I am free from sin and condemnation.

If I am free and cleansed from sin, *then* He dwells in me.

We can't control the outcomes of life through our striving. But *if* we give the control to God, *then* we can walk the sanctified path of "love, joy, peace, patience, kindness, goodness, faithfulness, gentleness, and self-control" (Galatians 5:22-23).

I'd love to let my friend Jaclyn Harwell tell you her own story of releasing control:

> Motherhood is the most terrifying, gut-wrenching, humbling endeavor a woman can endure. After all, it is my firm belief that God created parenthood, not to make us happy, but to bring us closer to Him, transform us into something *resembling Him.*
>
> There is joy, yes. But make no mistake, each scrap of joy feels hard won in the midst of toddler tantrums, piles of dirty dishes and laundry, and, for many families, behavioral and developmental disorders.
>
> My oldest was just three when we were told he needed to be on medication for his extreme case of ADHD. We resisted. From there, things got worse before they got better. We pressed on.
>
> Later, he developed sensory processing disorder (SPD) and oppositional defiant disorder (ODD), things that could not be disciplined away, not for my lack of trying.

The more I tried to discipline the defiance out of him, the angrier he got, and the angrier, more confused, and more frustrated I became.

Before I knew it, chaos ruled, and our home was a big ball of anger and resentment.

I resented my lot in life: his behavior and the loneliness it brought. (It's very difficult to make friends when your kid doesn't play well with other kids. Before long, people stop showing up for playdates…and you stop scheduling them.)

I became a "no" mom. "No, you can't get that paint out because you'll make a mess." "No, we can't go to that birthday party because the cake will contain food dye." Between our new strict diet and supplement routines, there was little room for fun.

When we said "no" to medication for our son, we were, in effect, committing to handling his symptoms naturally. And so began our long roller-coaster journey of healing ADHD, ODD, OCD, BPD, and the "D" responsible for them all: an increasingly common but poorly understood condition called PANDAS (pediatric autoimmune neuropsychiatric disorders associated with streptococcal infections).

We visited expensive doctors and tried to get help from pediatricians who didn't have the resources we needed, with minimal success. Still, we pressed on.

And then, something happened. We found the right combination of just the right supplements and just the right diet, and he began to change. His unreasonable anger vanished. Our home became more peaceful.

We even ate doughnuts, the ones with food dye, and he

didn't have a meltdown. It was glorious and freeing. But it was fleeting, as symptoms have since come and gone.

In the midst of all of it, I rested on my own knowledge, my own research, and my own works. I could fix him, because that's what moms do: We fix things. We fix our kids; we fix our husbands; we fix dinner every night. Why shouldn't I be able to handle something like ADHD?

I forgot that, ultimately, it's not by my own works I'll be saved, so certainly my children won't be saved by my works.

And even though we've come so far, each setback feels like a devastating blow. I question where *I* went wrong, why *I'm* not enough, and what I need to do to fix it.

When we're in a particularly challenging season of behavioral flares, my instinct is to research, to find a doctor or a new supplement that can help—when, in reality, the Creator of the universe, the Great Physician, is on *speed dial*.

I may not know in the hard seasons just what to do to help my son, but I do know the One who does, and He's teaching me to rest in knowing that. To rest in Him. Resting is something us mamas don't know nearly enough about. I'm learning to trust Him and lean not on *my own* understanding.

The good news is that as much as I love my son, God loves him exponentially more and wants more for him than I can ever dream or imagine. So, over and over, I remind myself to let go of my need for control, and over and over, I place him in God's hands. That's a pretty good place to be.

As I read Jaclyn's story, it was hard not to shake my head. *If only,* I thought. *If only I had known then...*

This journey is
not about being
a perfect parent.
It is about being
parented by a
perfect Father.

Chapter 3

PRETTY PICTURES

Be kind to each other, tenderhearted, forgiving one
another, just as God through Christ has forgiven you.

EPHESIANS 4:32

I've occasionally checked out a few of the current "easy meals in minutes" blogs. I read these for three reasons. First, I always strive to find better ways to feed my family. Second, I am fascinated by anyone who can write 900 words on refrigerator biscuit pizzas. Third, they affirm my personal belief in what is actually an easy meal in minutes—that is, of course, the five-dollar pizza.

Given the following two options, there is only one that makes sense to me:

> Take a can of refrigerator biscuits and flatten them out into individual "pizza" crusts. In several bowls, place pizza toppings; fill one bowl with pizza sauce and others with cheese, pepperoni, sausage, bell peppers, onions, and olives. Call your family to the dining room and allow them to create their own pizzas. When they have finished with their creations, bake for 10 to 12 minutes or until bubbly. Enjoy!

Or:

> Drive to Little Caesars and send teenage son in to buy
> five five-dollar Hot-N-Ready pizzas—three pepperonis
> and two cheeses. Argue with other teenage son about
> too many carbohydrates. Dig two dollars in quarters out
> of the cup holder and give in to his nagging. Send him
> into the store to get breadsticks. Eat breadsticks with
> happy children on the way home. Serve pizzas at home
> on paper plates. Enjoy!

Come on, refrigerator biscuit pizza? I have no words for the level
of inconvenience this "easy" meal would afford me.

Of course, the end of the blog post shows pictures of this stunning
family of four eating their personal biscuit pizzas and playing a board
game. Here is where Satan goes to town on me. He doesn't whisper; he yells, *You are such a loser! You and I both know the pieces to your
Monopoly game have been missing for years!* He's right. Last time we
even tried to play Monopoly, the box held only the board, a half-eaten
Oreo (I think it was an Oreo; I hope it was an Oreo), some pieces of
a puzzle of the Statue of Liberty, and a colossal mess of fake money.

Satan insinuates that moms who make little pizzas for their
babies preside over homes that are more sacred than mine. And I
believe him. So I buy another book or subscribe to another blog that
will help me be better so the ground beneath me will become sacred.

Lies.

The sacred ground of my home, where my children will learn
about Jesus Christ, where He dwells with us, has sticky floors. There
are drawings on the walls in crayon. There is a hole in the drywall
shaped suspiciously like a head, which appeared after the boys had
an impromptu wrestling match. There is laundry on the dining
room table, dishes in the sink. And I always strive to be better and
do better come Monday.

In my journey as mother, I have given up my dignity, my last french fry, and my whole heart. I now believe this journey we're on is not about being a perfect parent. It is about being parented by a perfect Father. It is about uncovering and trusting that perfect Parent so you *can* parent with your messes and flaws and be present for little human beings in want.

The enemy does not want you to believe in the sacred value of your home or mission. Mothers are inundated by his negativity and manipulative ways. Since the beginning, when Eve was tempted on the most sacred ground, Satan has slithered around while cheating, lying, and terrorizing womankind. This is his craft.

What I had missed for the longest time was this truth: God doesn't require us to be perfect (or perfectly ready) in order to be loved or used by Him. Mary, the mother of Jesus, was just a girl. Paul, the church's greatest evangelist, was a persecutor. David, the man after God's own heart, was just a boy. Moses, who delivered God's people from Egypt, was a murderer and a runaway who stuttered. Still, they trod on sacred ground.

World's Worst Supermom

Our son John's diagnosis went from being deaf to having auditory processing disorder—an umbrella for a variety of learning disabilities, specifically dyslexia. Unable to bear the idea of the most gentle creature I had ever met being criticized and labeled and regularly having to face the defeat of comparison, I convinced Justin we should withdraw Maggie from public school and start John in kindergarten at home. I was determined that homeschooling the children would protect them from a variety of hurts and discriminations. Certainly I would prove that hypothesis void, but that's another story.

The varying levels of peace that homeschooling afforded me led to a season I adored. The day we pulled away from Maggie's school with her nap mat and number-two pencils in a paper sack, I felt the clock stall. I seemed to believe that the public education system clicked off days until the end of my role as a mother. I tossed grades and assessments out the window. John was oblivious to how "behind" he was. More than anything in the world, I wanted him to be well. I wanted him to be able to learn and retain what he learned.

I added his struggle to my failures. His problems defined me. So I became "super homeschool mom."

I was a one-woman schoolhouse. I woke the children before dawn and prayed with them. We ate free-range, hard-boiled eggs and drank organic smoothies and chanted Latin derivatives and sang history songs. We dissected frogs, grew lima beans in Dixie cups, watched the History channel, and waited for the bowls with avocado seeds and toothpicks on the window sill to do something, anything. We ate spinach salad for dinner and drove from the ranch into town for swim team at night.

At least, that was how it looked from the outside. But Luke was now having uncontrollable difficulties. His fits of rage and crying lasted anywhere from six to ten hours at a time, and they had our home life and marriage in shambles.

Eventually Luke was diagnosed with an adrenaline disorder. It turned out that he produced excessive amounts of adrenaline and then cried to spend it, which only produced more.

Even with therapy, Luke was hard to deal with. He was unhappy, and surely this was a reflection of me as a mother. I said and did things I never thought I'd say or do. Suggestions from outsiders on how to deal with him were relentless. On the rare occasion we were all out in public and he went into a fit of rage, the jeers and stares provided justification for the list of inabilities and atrocities I believed about myself. I sank deeper into my identity as World's Worst Mom.

To this day, I remember the look on my Luke's face when I

walked into the preschool office and found him sitting in a corner (this was after a mother's day out and before we started homeschooling). It is burned in my memory. He had lost control in front of his peers, his beloved teacher, and one of the moms. He was humiliated and mystified. He ran into my arms when he saw me, whimpering, "I so sorry. I so sorry, Mommy."

Luke's suffering was real. Onlookers may have seen an out-of-control brat. They might have accused me of being a poor disciplinarian or a horrible mother, but *I knew him.* Behind his brokenhearted green eyes was the wisest and most compassionate child I had ever met. He was kind; he was observant. He was never deliberately hateful or intentionally out of control.

In the preschool office, I overheard a teacher whisper, "That kid needs a bustin' soon. What are his parents thinking?"

For a moment, I felt unworthy to be a parent. But it occurred to me that my heavenly Father is not defined by my meltdowns. Why should my value be decided by how my kids behave one day to the next? Just as I can't take credit for their shining moments, I can't carry the weight of all my children's failings and breakdowns—but I can share it, and I can help them take it all to Jesus.

That day, when Luke and I were both made to feel ashamed, I wish I had said, "God will use this boy in ways you cannot comprehend." Instead, I took my son home early, and we ate ice cream together for lunch and cuddled in bed. I wept silent prayers of restoration over him as he drifted off to sleep.

We were both broken, and we were both so loved by our God.

These days, we call such moments "mom shaming." It is a terrible thing. From behind our laptop screens, it is easy to voice our distaste for moms who breastfeed in public or show up with a child missing the proper-weighted coat. Allow me to warn you: Never say never. Like, ever. These things you are so certain you would never do could be the very things that get you through the line at the grocery store.

Here is the most valuable piece of parenting advice I can offer you: Freely admit your child would and can do anything. You see a six-year-old with a pacifier? Your response: "Well, at least he's quiet!" A pregnant thirteen-year-old? "Someone gets to be a young grandparent!" But never, ever, say never.

Moms grow guilt like placenta and back fat. It comes naturally. We don't need our issues pointed out to us on Facebook. Almost all of us are fully aware we are doing it wrong. But here's the beautiful truth: We don't answer to one another. We only answer to the One who sees the whole picture—the One who created us.

Our journeys,
unique as each
of us, have to be
trusted to a God
who fully loves.

Chapter 4

GREENER GRASS

*If I want him to remain alive until I return, what
is that to you? As for you, follow me.*

JOHN 21:22

I sat across from the broken couple and listened to their apprehensions. I didn't know them well, but I was honored to answer their questions about the adoption process. The woman held a worried-worn piece of paper that was covered, front and back, in questions. As she went through her list, her voice cracked with the ache of an empty womb. Infertility is not an issue I have dealt with. I cannot pretend I understand; I can only imagine the depths of this hurt. And this woman was in pain. Finally, she broke.

"I just wanted so much to experience the natural aspects of becoming a mother," she said.

I don't know why my friend was barren. Again, I don't assume to understand her heartache. This woman has the heart of a mother, and her desire to nurture and care for another human being was a legitimate and passionate expression of how well she loves.

I told her I was sorry. And as a biological and adoptive mother,

I wanted her to know two things. First, the most unnatural thing that has *ever* happened to my body is pregnancy and childbirth. Second, the most beautiful, most glorious birthing experience of my life had been adoption.

"When you are handed your first child," I told her, "this journey will start to make sense to you. When you are handed your second or third, the mystery will further unravel. God knows the cries of your heart, and He will answer with children that He chose for you. Biology is actually a pretty simple form of becoming a parent. You will become a mother in the same design that God has chosen us as sons and daughters: adoption."

This precious woman was looking around her, comparing herself to the other women she saw, and felt that if she couldn't give birth the same way they did, she was somehow *less than*. Thoughts such as, *Why can't I do things this way? Everyone else is doing it!* leave us broken and depleted. Our journeys, unique as each of us, have to be trusted to a God who fully loves.

Thief of Joy

At the heart of so many women's grief and struggle is the enemy of comparison. And it starts at the very beginning of motherhood.

She can have children. I can't.

She can breastfeed. I can't get my son to latch on.

She gave birth naturally. I had to have a C-section.

These are words that leave us depleted and feeling less than loved by the Father who adores us. The pain caused by these harmful words—even the words that don't travel any farther than our minds—is real, and their power continues to amaze me. Here, before we've barely become mothers, we start looking around and finding ourselves wanting.

Worse, we look around and find *others* wanting. While feeling "less than" in some areas, we're happy to stand in judgment of people in others. Take the birthing process, for instance. If you want to experience the wrath of the internet, try telling it what you think about the best way to deliver a baby.

I have opinions about this, of course. I've given birth "naturally," and I didn't like anything about it. On a scale of one to ten, my pain threshold is a negative nine. I gauge a paper cut at an eight. And what part of "positive strep throat culture" doesn't warrant a morphine drip? So, this is how I feel about a human erupting from a tiny space on my person: It *hurts*. That pain is real. And whatever you can do to lessen that pain is a good thing.

But my opinions are about what worked for me. So even though I think the idea of birthing children into an inflatable swimming pool in your living room is unnatural—and I can say that because inflatable swimming pools do not occur in nature—it's not up to me. Whatever floats your afterbirth. We were created as individual daughters, and my preference does not have to be yours. Birth that baby where you want to. Do what you will with your placenta—freeze-dry it, make it into a hat, whatever. That is your prerogative. But let us allow one another to have these choices.

Unfortunately, comparison doesn't stop at the birthing process. It can steal our joy at every stage of the parenting experience—from the baby years up through adulthood.

I want to be better at everything—like her. I want to be a better mom. I want to be a better wife. I want to be a better daughter, sister, friend, writer, and believer. I want to be moving forward in my career, like she is. I want my jeans to zip up—just like hers. There's gum in my hair—and it's not even my gum. She never has gum in her hair. Her kid can spell Mississippi; my kid sounds out "the." She only speaks to her kid in French; my kid has a french fry shoved up her nose. Her kid reads his Bible; my kid set the church library on fire. Her kid graduated summa cum laude; my kid was suspended.

Comparison can turn molehills into mountains, and the art of contrast becomes a slippery slope. I have found myself on this downhill slide more often than not.

Catfights and Cliques: Sports for All Ages

We had a short-term foster placement, Bella, staying at my home recently. Bella has long, brown, flowing curls. During her stay with us, another child, Joy-Baby, came for a visit. I've known Joy-Baby since she was an infant, and not once have I seen her lash out at anyone. But Joy-Baby's blue eyes met Bella's brown ones and narrowed. She walked right up to Bella and violently pulled her hair.

It starts young. And unfortunately, it doesn't end.

This was brought home to me at a recent Mother's Day event. I was speaking to a group of elderly women at an upscale assisted living community. While I was waiting to speak, I sat at a table near the podium. A group of 80-somethings came rolling in on power scooters. The formation reminded me of a biker gang. A couple of people waved and yelled, "Hi!" in the direction of the motorized grannies.

The clique ignored them.

As the room filled, a single chair remained empty at the "gang's" table. A well-dressed woman with a cane glanced about the room and spied the chair. She shuffled toward them, and I watched her address them. "Well hello, new friends!" she said. "It would be a pleasure to sit with you!"

One of the scooter babes dropped a huge purple purse in the empty chair, and the leader said, "Taken." They then began to talk among themselves, ignoring the sweet, seatless woman.

I pulled out a chair for her. She said, "Oh my, thank you! I am new here! Are you the guest speaker?"

"Yes, I am." *How sweet,* I thought. And then she turned in her seat, stuck out her tongue at the gang, and said, "Maybe I'll get her autograph for you."

My jaw dropped. My sophomore year of high school reverberated in my brain, and I was slain with the gut-wrenching reality that I am going to meet crazed, jealous, comparative females from toddlerhood to the grave.

You can't stop people from judging and comparing themselves to you, forming cliques and terrorizing one another with *better than– less than* attitudes, but you can choose to stop doing it to yourself. You can let the buck stop with you. Give yourself a break; let Jesus lord over you.

Compassion over Comparison

Recently, while out shopping with my younger daughter, Sophie, we witnessed a mother struggling to get through the store checkout while dealing with a little boy in meltdown mode. He had huge brown eyes and soft, brown, curly hair. By his behavior, I surmised he lived with something like autism. A beautiful boy, throwing a ghastly fit. The mother was a mess of sweat and tears. The items in her cart were necessities, but we could tell her regret for having attempted the outing was reaching a tipping point.

I heard her plead with the boy. "Please, let's just check out, and I will buy you a sucker."

Then I heard an older man behind us scoff. "That's his problem," the man said. "He needs a beating, not a reward."

Sophie and I sprang into action. "Don't listen to him!" I barked— loud enough that the man could hear me. "*You* know what it takes to get through the day and help your boy. Let us help you." Immediately, another female shopper unwrapped a sucker for the child, while Sophie and I unloaded items from the grocery cart onto the checkout belt. We worked together to get the woman and her distraught son to the car. Thankfully, this was a moment when I and a few others were able to help a mom in need. Empathy appeared before judgment could.

Wouldn't it be great if empathy were always the first response? Personally, I have so many experiences to confess in my own parental journey that if empathy and *I totally understand* aren't my first thoughts, then I'm not trying to listen to the other person's story. But it seems to all come back to judgment and comparison.

We all have moments when we are bargaining and begging with our child or ourselves to get through another day or a checkout line. I recall one day when I took Maggie to the emergency room for a temper tantrum. No, really. She wanted this doll, and I couldn't afford it. She lost her ever-loving mind. She was blue in the face, stark raving mad. I had never seen her act like that, and I could feel all these judgmental eyes on me. It was so outside the realm of normal Maggie behavior that I thought she had developed a tumor. So, I took her to the ER.

The ER is kind of like the confessional of nonsensical mompanic episodes. We go there when common sense and terror collide. I fully expect to someday uncover a hidden camera that allows other beings in the universe to watch my motherhood antics that occurred in random emergency rooms throughout Texas, some parts of New Mexico, and once in Utah. Kind of like *I Love Lucy* for extraterrestrials in the galaxy.

The ER is that place in which every mother will eventually find herself racked with terror when these humans who call us "Mom" fall prey to this destination called "life."

When I brought Maggie to the ER, Justin and my mother-in-law rushed to my side. We held vigil and prayed and waited for the test results. When the doctor entered the room, I braced myself for the worst.

"Ma'am, it appears your daughter just really wanted that Tropical Splash Barbie," the doctor said.

I think I was hoping her tantrum was caused by a physical ailment and not just…sinful behavior. Ugh, there it is. Our babies have a sin nature. The least we can do is have compassion on the other parents we see in the thick of it.

Defined by Our Stories

Our little foster-love Bella was injured when she arrived in our care. She had a thigh-high, hot-pink cast. For the first few days, we stayed around the house. The cast was cumbersome, and although she was an easygoing child, she tired easily.

After a week of her officially being in our care, I decided to brave an outing to Walmart with her and our two adopted sons, Sam and Charlie—whom we call "the Vandals."

Here's a picture of our crew that day:

Sam has a dark complexion—his beautiful skin is like melted caramel—with jet-black hair and onyx eyes. Charlie is blond with golden-hazel eyes and rosy cheeks the texture of butter. They are altogether gorgeous. My sister fondly refers to them as SPF 10 and SPF 50, as Sam only gets browner in the sun, and Charlie needs a scuba suit so as not to get crispy when he's by the pool.

Our new little friend is probably an SPF 15. She's exotic. Her eyes are, somehow, simultaneously blue, green, brown, and gold. I have never seen anything like them. She has naturally curly brown hair and incredible, perfectly shaped rosebud-red lips.

As I pushed the children through the store in the shopping cart, an older woman stopped me and commented on their loveliness. They warrant attention. They are gorgeous.

And I, with my messy hair bun and ragged yoga pants, am typically disheveled. I mean, I'm not a total mess—I don't scare sheep or anything. Still, since that first outing to the store with Bella, like clockwork, someone in another line or right behind me makes remarks to their shopping mate about the origin of my children and my slothfulness, in that order, usually with a nod to food stamps.

"Wow, she's popular with the fellas."

Or, "That woman has herself a handful of baby daddies."

I grit my teeth and keep pushing the cart. *They don't know. They don't get it. They're judging because they don't understand.*

I didn't speak up the first time someone made a comment about me and my multicolored family, and it wasn't the first time, or the last. I didn't whirl around and explain our situation ever so sweetly. Nor have I spoken up any day since. Of all the times I've been judged in a grocery store for my babies of different colors, I've never said a word.

This is not cowardice. This is a stance. Those who speak or sneer their hateful judgments are not going to hear my story. And they will definitely not hear the stories of the precious, rambunctious children hanging on to my shopping cart. The kids' histories are theirs to tell. The people at the store only see what they want to see, so they don't get to rejoice in the awesomeness of these kids and their remarkable, God-given stories of restoration.

We judge and are judged. We pick people apart, forming opinions based on no information at all, and we let those opinions divide us.

Oh, sweet Mama, you are doing just fine. Don't look to the right or the left. Don't stand in want of something she has, and don't stand in judgment of what she is lacking. Instead, pray for her. You and the woman beside you have a common bond: You love like no other. The ground beneath you both is sacred.

**Believing God
is the catalyst
for doing
brave things.**

Chapter 5

FEAR FACTORY

*I am leaving you with a gift—peace of mind and
heart. And the peace I give is a gift the world
cannot give. So don't be troubled or afraid.*

JOHN 14:27

Terror, an inevitable and frequent guest of mothers. God did not give me a spirit of fear, but if He graced me with children, certainly He knew I would develop that spirit and would spend the rest of my days trying to resolve it.

Years after that emergency room visit where Maggie was diagnosed with a passionate want of a Barbie, she decided to study abroad for college. I was happy for her, but I also worried about what it would be like to worry about her on the other side of the big pond. Prior to her departure, I would sit upright in bed in the wee hours, horrified at the size of the planet.

I would think, *I just can't. What if…and what then?*

These were the words I thought and spoke most often. I was in bondage to my worries. And I worried about how *much* I worried. If

I really believed, I shouldn't be this worried, right? I was on a merry-go-round of terror with no merriment, constantly thinking about accidents that may or may not befall the ones I loved.

Perhaps we have too much to think about, too much brain space and power spent on way too many falsehoods. When we worry, we're missing out on the blessings of a good God. When our focus is on our fear, it's not on the Savior. We're forgetting to peek behind the mirror of our self to see the stash of peace He has for us.

The enemy wants you to believe untrue things about your heavenly Father. The more wrong, the better. He wants you to believe that God is passing out bedbugs, cancer, and car crashes. Sweet sister, He is not out to get you, me, or our babies. He is crazy in love with us, and we can turn to truth when bad things happen:

> "I know the plans I have for you," says the LORD. "They are plans for good and not for disaster, to give you a future and a hope. In those days when you pray, I will listen. If you look for me wholeheartedly, you will find me. I will be found by you," says the LORD, "I will end your captivity" (Jeremiah 29:11-14).

Here's the beautiful thing: The future the prophet speaks of here is our future with Christ in heaven. This is our God. This is our hope. He brings us out of the captivity of fear, stands us on solid ground, and points us toward His perfect promises.

The accumulation of fears I have is definitely exponential. But when I examine them, 99 percent of them revolve around my children. It's not my own life I dwell on—it's theirs. At my core, fear has been a determining factor in my life and faith; it only grew when I was first called "Mom." But looking at fear with fresh eyes could be the substance to a renewed sense of how good God is—and the peaceful good night's sleep you have been craving.

A Learned Response

You were not born with a spirit of fear. This is not the nature you were given, nor were your children born with this character. We teach it, or we learn it when an event occurs that instills it within us.

Recently I had an early flight to Canada. Justin needed to take care of the other children, so I asked Luke, seventeen at the time, to take me to the airport. It was a little after six in the morning, still dark. Luke was barely awake. I drove and hoped and quietly prayed he would be coherent by the time we arrived at the airport, so he could drive back home safely.

As we made our way out of our neighborhood, I noticed a girl with long black hair standing under a streetlight. She had on a backpack and was holding a lunch box. Obviously, she was waiting for the school bus.

Luke stirred in his seat and opened his eyes long enough to notice the girl. And then he started flailing and screaming. With his seat belt still buckled, he scampered into the back seat, hollering, "Noooo! Help! Noooo!"

I nearly drove into a neighbor's yard, swerved to miss a mailbox, and then brought the car safely to a stop up on a curb. Unable to even fathom what had caused my son to curl into a fetal position in the back seat, one foot tangled in the front seat belt, I asked him what was wrong. He panted, "Why is that little girl standing in the light?"

Bewildered, I explained, "Because she's waiting for the bus."

His muscles relaxed, and he inhaled deeply, grasping one hand over his pounding heart. "Oh. Wow. That was terrifying."

What part of a little girl waiting for her ride to school can make a young man all but wet his pants? The learned fear of a little girl climbing out of a well and wandering down dark and murderous halls. Yes, Luke and Sophie's favorite pastime is watching horror flicks. He was not born afraid of little girls standing in the light of a lamppost. But he has been so traumatized, albeit in a self-inflicted way, that this is now his legitimate nightmare.

On our ranch, it's necessary for us to instill the fear of rattlesnakes into our wandering children. However, it isn't until you come up on one and hear that notorious rattle and see the flash of deadly fangs that you are truly afraid of *ever* coming upon one again. A learned and somewhat healthy response. So, while we are not given a spirit of fear by our Creator, some fears are of benefit. But others rob us of peace and joy, that which our Creator died to give us.

I used to try to negotiate with God. *If I do good things, maybe He won't let bad things happen to my children.* If this were how God moved, then paying your tithe would be a foolproof tactic for a life free from fear. How many "good" Christians do you know who have lost a child in a tragic accident or to an illness? Our good works do not motivate God to act. Changing your mind about this, the idea that good or bad behavior impacts God's care of you or your babies, is paramount to walking in the freedom of your inheritance, dear friend.

God is of one nature: good. He can't be anything but good. Which means He is not the author of tragedy. He is the author of life, and life abundant. Yes, He may allow trial. He may not answer a prayer, a genuine plea for help, the way you want Him to, but He is still good. His will? His will was and is Jesus.

The statement, "We are praying for God's will," lends a note of terror. As if we are playing Russian roulette, and this crazed, mad man-god could start passing out lymphoma. But when we understand that God's will is Jesus, we realize that He is a God of mercy.

He gave His will, His only Son, as sacrifice for your sons and daughters.

In a recent interview, I was asked how I was able to face the impending removal of a long-term foster-love, Joy-baby. When the interview was posted, it was accompanied by a quote from me:

"Believing God is the catalyst for doing brave things." I thought it was a misprint. I went back and listened. Sure enough, I said it.

And you know what? I believe.

I believe God is a good Father. I believe He loves me. I believe nothing can separate me from that love. When and how did this change come about in me? When I stopped believing my works motivated Him.

What do you want your children to believe about you? That they can trust you? That you will provide for them? That you love them unconditionally? And what must they do to earn that trust, provision, and love? When they woke up this morning, what did they have to do to be your child? Nothing. That is who they are; their identity is being your child. In a healthy relationship, there is no fear of losing that role.

Believe God.

Believe He loves you, died for you, cannot be separated from you.

Believe His will is Jesus.

Believe the plans He has for you.

Believe that when you're walking through the valley of the shadow of death—and you will—He will go with you. No matter if you cussed, skipped church, or ate Cheez-Its and pie for dinner. The antidote to fear isn't to become *more* of His child; the antidote to fear is to believe you *are* His child.

Our son John—who is no fun to watch horror flicks with because he doesn't jump, startle, or scream when things leap out on the screen—is annoyingly fearless. One evening he and a couple of friends were going to sleep in our hunting cabin, way out in the woods of our ranch. I overheard them talking about renting a movie. John suggested, "Hey! Let's rent *The Cabin in the Woods*! I heard it's really scary!"

His friends thought this was a terrible idea and refused. When John asked why, one friend replied, "Dude, we are literally going to be spending the night *in a cabin in the woods.*"

John, who wanders the ranch barefoot in the middle of the night, has a next-level bravery I admire, and yet it horrifies me. Once, I asked him about it. "Why aren't you afraid wandering around in the dark at night alone?" I asked.

I recall he was leaning against the kitchen counter, gnawing on an entire English cucumber. He shrugged complacently and said, "What's to be afraid of? I know how it ends, and I know who wins."

Oh, but to truly believe.

If I could

control any of this,

I would keep my

children out of

harm's way. But

keeping them safe

would deny them

a chance to serve.

Chapter 6

I SO PROUD YOU IS SMART

Joyful is the person who finds wisdom,
the one who gains understanding.

PROVERBS 3:13

Her name, Sophia, means "wisdom."

Born with Luke's face and a head full of silky, jet-black hair that stood straight on end, she was an enchanting, mystical pixie. Immediately after her delivery, I had an emergency hysterectomy. She slept with me and nursed (my most successful breastfed baby) while I healed. She was the perfect companion. But early on, we suspected she was a little bit sharper than the other tools in the shed.

The first hard proof of Sophie's "abilities" took place on New Year's Eve, when Sophie was about 18 months old. Gathered around my parents' dining room table after dinner, we played cards and chatted about our New Year's resolutions. As always, we discussed diets, exercise, things we "just must quit," and accomplishments that weighed heavy on our to-do lists. Sophie sat at a child-sized table with a pacifier in her mouth, coloring in a *Pirates of the Caribbean* coloring book.

Without so much as a word, Sophie stood up, toddled over to the table, and handed me her pacifier. A few minutes later, she delivered a bottle and her baby blanket to me. Later, when I tucked her into bed, I tried to give her the pacifier, blanket, and a fresh bottle. She shook her head no and rolled over. Not only did she wean herself off the infantile items, but the next morning I found her sitting on the toilet. She never had an accident. The child potty trained herself.

From the time she was two, she could play the piano by ear. Poor Maggie would come bolting from the bathtub, suds in her hair and wrapped in a soaking towel, screaming, "Sophie! Not my recital piece!" Truly, there is little as insulting as spending hours trying to perfect "Tale as Old as Time" for your fourth-grade concert, only to have your toddler sister knock it out in seconds while drinking chocolate milk from a Baby Einstein sippy cup. She added insult to injury by singing along like Céline Dion.

Sophie memorized all of her siblings' times tables and Latin derivatives before kindergarten, and she taught herself to ride a bike while her bewildered older bothers stood next to their "big kid" bikes with training wheels. The kid could even *juggle*, while her peers attempted to stack blocks.

Quite honestly, we are still a little scared of Sophie. When she was nine, a commercial for the horror movie *The Exorcism of Emily Rose* came on television. Maggie, John, and Luke all squealed, "We have to see that!"

Without looking up from her macaroni and cheese, Sophie said, "Don't bother. I saw it. It is ridiculous."

"What?" I gasped, "It's rated R!"

Sophie scoffed. "R for ridiculous."

"Who did you watch it with?" I pleaded, hoping maybe Justin in an insomniac state had agreed to watch it with her.

"No one. I watched it alone the other night when I couldn't sleep."

"How did you unlock my password to see an R-rated movie?"

"I surmised it was your birthday or Dad's. It was yours."

Y'all, she *surmises* things?

It's little things like this that have us sleeping with one eye open. We're afraid to make her mad, because what if she can start a fire with her mind?

And her memory recall? My parents call her to ask for their Wi-Fi password. Chills crawl up and down my spine each time I hear her on the phone saying, "Oh, hi Papa! Yes, it's LHNMH665943T-GHNI?//. No problem. Love you too!" Did I drink nuclear waste or get too close to a power line when I was pregnant with her? If this is the product of breastfeeding, let it be said, breastfeed, for the love!

All this to say, the more Sophie's brain feeds off digital encyclopedias and calculations for black holes and supernovas, the less I am able to recognize my identity in her. Frankly, to be championed for Sophie's accomplishments is the greatest of ill-received compliments. We don't know what happened that afforded her these powers. She just won an award in algebra. Algebra! This isn't something Justin and I can pride ourselves in.

Maggie worked tirelessly to achieve her B times in swimming competitions, while at his first meet, John dove in the pool and scored an AA time. John studied countless hours for a Latin exam and failed, while Luke, who never cracked a book, made straight *A*s.

John couldn't read when he was nine, but if someone asked him a question, he would answer "sir" or "ma'am" before addressing them. We didn't teach him that. When John was 11, my dad made a deal with Turkmenistan for his company. When we told the kids that Papa had successfully negotiated with the Turks, John laughed and said, "Wow, not even the Crusaders were able to negotiate with the Turks."

Right.

Not my doing. They are who they are. And they are God's kids. The whole crew, from my firstborn to the foster-loves who keep my floors sticky. (They, by the way, are beautiful, but I never know what to say when someone tells me so: "Um…thanks? I cannot take credit for their appearance. I just met this child.")

Fragile Success

I've rebelled against the idea of taking credit for or bragging about my children. Maybe because I found it embarrassing when other people did it. Or maybe because of John's disabilities, grappling with the understanding that I couldn't take responsibility for my kids' gifts *or* their weaknesses.

It wasn't easy to do this because, as much as I was in awe of Sophie's mind, I was equally consumed with John's struggles. I wanted to be able to fix him at all costs, and it was wearing thin on everyone in our family. Against my better judgment and even my beliefs, I was clinging to a standard of what *normal* looked like. And I was blaming myself that we weren't living that out. I believed our family's imperfections were all my fault.

What part of my kids' accomplishments is about me? Why should I be praised when they win the state chess tournament or ostracized when they are arrested for shoplifting? Where do they stop and I begin?

This, I feel, was the lie that kept me in bondage, that somehow my children's accomplishments added to my redemption, and their failures took from it. The salvation of a mom in this manner seems far-fetched, but think about it. If you are strapped to a works-based theology, if you are doing all the "things"—up at 5:00 to study the Word, church on Wednesday and twice on Sunday, the potluck, the quilting bee, a baby shower, and life group—and your child drops an f-bomb during choir practice…who repents?

Often, it's Mom.

At my best "Christianese," I was saying and doing all the things. At my worst? I overheard my older kids say, "Agnostic." And, "I just don't believe that he could have survived in a whale." And, "They lied about Santa? Why would I believe them about this?" Crushed, terrified, and repentant, I fully believed I had failed in every aspect of my motherhood and my Christianhood. And this lie only perpetuated the great divide between me and my Father.

I spent John's entire childhood trying to protect him. I took him off the short bus and sat him at the kitchen table, safe in my home. We did phonics until our eyes bled. He sounded out "the…eeee…hhhhh…tttt" until I would sob. Just "the." *The.* I poured into that boy and begged God to set him free from his "disabilities."

Not long ago, he climbed onto a bus for marine boot camp and a span of days when he was exposed to constant verbal abuse. They hollered at him and called him an idiot. He confessed, "The first week, all I could think was, *They'll send me home because I never can get my right and left correct.*"

My heart ached at the thought of this. I reverted back to feeling responsible for protecting him. Taking care of that man-baby was my mission, and I was failing. When he told me about the written-test portion of camp, I ached for him. There was just no way. Ten seconds to read the question projected on the wall and then answer it on a Scantron sheet. Every dyslexic person's worst testing nightmare.

He got a score of 98 out of 100.

How We Love

I've learned a lot from 1 Corinthians 13.

Love is patient, even when the kid can't get past the word *the.*

Love rejoices, but it does not boast in the kids' accomplishments.

Love protects, but it does not pad the kids' knees and elbows when they cross the street.

Here in Texas, it is pretty easy to find an example of prideful love. Our football gods have their numbers strewn across our tailgates, our coaches are fired if we don't make it to state, and "our" players somehow define us.

But who am I to be proud? What did I accomplish in my children? How many times did I tell John, "We don't blow things up, mister!" Now he's a small-weapons engineer. I told him, "Don't play with fire." Now he's a rifle expert. I told him over and over and over, "You may not swim with your shoes on!" And he just earned a swimming recognition…in his combat boots.

I would like to say it's enough that I nurtured when nurturing was needed. I loved well, fearlessly. But that barely seems to scratch the surface. What I want and what I can control are not in the same camp.

If I could control any of this, I would keep my children out of harm's way. But keeping them safe would deny them a chance to serve. And keeping myself safe would deny me the same opportunities.

Two years ago, in a nondescript hotel room, I committed myself to a stranger's child. If I am to be totally honest, it was an apology of sorts. Earlier that evening Justin had been walking the floor with the new foster placement, singing George Strait songs to soothe her. My gut lurched. He was totally smitten. The warning caught in my throat, "Justin…" He swayed to meet my eyes, "What?"

I hesitated. "It's just, uh, don't…" His eyes narrowed. He knew what I was thinking, and despite the glare, and how much I hated it when others said it to me, I said it anyway. "Just be careful, she probably won't stay very long. Don't…" He stopped me. "Don't what, Jami? Don't fall in love, don't love her too much? This little girl will be loved *fearlessly*, no matter what." He returned to comforting her. I knew he was right.

Later that night when the infant woke to be fed, I sat in the corner of the dimly lit hotel room, barely illuminated by the neighboring Taco Bell sign. Justin was right. Who was I not to pick up this cross and love fearlessly? I whispered to the baby girl snuggled in my arms, "I will love you, and you will have my whole heart, no matter how much it hurts." Now, I'm discovering just *how much* that love hurts. Her biological mother has made choices, has made changes, and is ready to receive her daughter into her arms.

I don't want to say goodbye. But would I take back my promise if I could? What would I have said? "I'll love you, but only a little." "I'll give you my heart, but not too much of it." Could I look into the eyes of a young mother and pray for her destruction, so I could be rewarded with the child she gave birth to?

Nope. Couldn't do it.

I So Glad You Is You

My son gives away his last five dollars to a homeless man on the street…and leaves his car to walk back to the dorm in freezing rain, because he has no gas money.

My daughter walks the floor with our foster-love, singing lullabies, adoring fully, knowing that very soon her empty arms will equate to a broken heart, a sister missed.

Justin, the man of my dreams, nearly fifty, sits on a canyon bluff teaching his adopted toddler sons about the land they will learn to plow, sow, and cultivate.

I know I need to release my kids—not just the foster-loves, but all my children—to God's care. This pounding head and hurting heart will have no choice then but to call on my Jesus, the greatest conclusion, the most delightful and costly decision I have ever had to make. Would I change this story? I would not. It is He who dwells in every corner of these dear hearts. He who will accomplish every good deed.

I can say to each child, "I'm so glad you are you." And to God, I can most certainly, wholeheartedly say, "I'm so glad You are You."

While we're
lost in our pain,
we can be sure
God is busy
faithfully making
plans for us.

Chapter 7

GRIEFTASTIC

Don't worry about anything; instead, pray about everything. Tell God what you need, and thank him for all he has done. Then you will experience God's peace, which exceeds anything we can understand. His peace will guard your hearts and minds as you live in Christ Jesus.

PHILIPPIANS 4:6-7

I have been to my share of funerals.

I remember standing in the foyer of the church on the morning of a family member's funeral when an older woman came up next to me and said, "I'm so sorry for your loss. You'd be wise to take stock of how you're living; God must be trying to show you something."

My brother-in-law, she believed, had died prematurely so that I could learn a lesson. Did I grow from having loved and lost him? Yes. But God doesn't kill people to teach other people not to max out their credit cards or to enjoy life to the fullest. My children's beloved uncle wasn't the sacrificial lamb—Jesus was.

People say things like this because they're looking for meaning in the midst of tragedy. If it can just be *for* something, have some purpose, then maybe it will make sense.

But death is always senseless. Jesus didn't promise to make it tidier or to give it some kind of reason or significance. He promised to overturn it, to undo it.

Oh well, you say. *It must have been God's will.*

God's will isn't premature death—His original design for us never included death. God's will is for the restoration of all things. We have a God who will hear us and help us through anything. He is not some criminal mastermind testing the strength of His people. And when you do suffer, you have this promise: He is with you.

The first time it dawned on me how misleading and hurtful some of our false beliefs and offhand sympathetic comments can be, I was at the funeral for a five-year-old boy named Brock. He'd died of brain cancer. My daughter Sophie was also five at the time.

The raw emotion of that funeral still haunts me—there was so much pain. That little coffin was a dozen different levels of wrong. His mom, Barb, looked as if she was commanding her body to perform its most basic function. Breathe. Breathe. Breathe. Because if she stopped reminding herself, her other children would be orphaned.

Barb had diligently cared for Brock, as any mother would, but she embraced her role as mother and a pediatric nurse with a level of dignity and wisdom that amazed and inspired. And although she grieved, I knew she still believed.

None of our trite sayings about death made any sense that day. Everything happens for a reason? God must have wanted another angel?

The grief of losing an older child to death has not been part of my story. The miscarriage of Luke's twin was painful and brought with it a lot of what-ifs and if-onlys. More recently, we lost a long-term foster placement whom we'd been trying to adopt, and her departure was agonizing. But seeing your five-year-old son in a coffin—I have no words. Walking that treacherous path is beyond me. The grief of missing, the ache of an empty future—my prayers are all I have to offer.

But I know that no matter the circumstances, God remains.

Yes, God is mysterious. But whether we face disappointment over an unreceived gift or a longed-for child or feel grief, loneliness, or despair, God has not forgotten us. Have we forgotten all He's done for us, all He is able to do? While we're lost in our pain, we can be sure He's busy faithfully making plans for us.

We pray to a God who only gives good things. We can't always understand how He heals or blesses—no one can—but He is always good. When we pass up the polite, formulaic words at funerals and instead run headlong into the real promises of resurrection, we and our messes and tumbles and losses are not met with the cold law, but with the warm embrace of our redeeming Lord. He is always a comforter. He is always a good Father.

Misplaced Blame

In 2012, Justin came home and told me that his mom, Iris, was dying. Her breast cancer had metastasized. She was declining quickly.

We moved from our large home on the ranch into a smaller house in town so Iris could have help from hospice, since the workers couldn't travel out to the ranch. Iris, who had lived alone in her own home on the ranch, never argued or questioned the move. We were all fully aware that this was the end of her journey on earth.

This house was modest but convenient for our needs at the time. I hired a lady to help me once a week with the house and with Iris's needs. We were barely settled, so the cleaning lady was a huge deal for me, a lifesaver. I couldn't keep up with Iris, the kids, the house, and homeschooling by myself. She was an old church friend of the family, and she really cared about my mother-in-law's comfort.

But things got weird quickly. This old church friend went from Florence Nightingale to Bonnie Parker faster than Clyde could pick a pocket. At the end of each weekly visit, the boys would come running to my room. "She did it again! She stole all our bathroom stuff!"

I would go and look, and sure enough, the teenage boys' tooth-brushes, toothpaste, shaving cream, hair products, brushes, cologne, and deodorant were gone.

This utterly stumped me. It would have made more sense for her to steal the girls' stuff. *If she's stealing, why take Axe products?* Justin suggested the boys' bathroom might be so disgusting that she was just throwing it all away. I wanted to believe that possibility more than the idea that she was stealing hygiene products.

I didn't have it in me to confront her. Instead, I kept buying replacements, and the ritual of disappearing toiletries continued. I was starting to doubt her now. She knew we were struggling. What could have been provoking her odd behavior?

One afternoon, I went into the boys' bathroom and started pull-ing open drawers and digging through cabinets, determined to solve the mystery. I bent over to look in the trash, and when I stood up, I smacked my head on the mirror above the sink. Click. The mirror opened. It was, in fact, a medicine cabinet.

Inside were *all* of the boys' toiletries.

I know. Hilarious. In our defense, we hadn't lived in the house long, and the cabinet was recessed, so the mirror was flat against the wall.

Call me crazy (it won't be the first time), but this reminds me of God storing up grace when we are misunderstanding Him. While we keep misplacing our knowledge of His love and mercy, He is faithfully storing up what we need, what we're looking for, and what has been hidden from us in our darker days.

There are many believers who show evidence of misplaced trust. "Church people speak" was a huge contributor to my belief I was not special, not loved or cared for by God. For example, take the statement, "God won't give you more than you can handle." So, when things get hard, when we have way more than we can handle, we doubt that He could be for us. We cry, "Why me? Why are You doing this to us?"

I know now what I wish I'd known long ago: When circumstances threaten to overwhelm you, He isn't doing it *to* you. He isn't cruel. He is grieving with you.

When you are crumbling under the weight of a loss or burden, stop telling yourself it isn't more than you can handle. You do need help. You *do* need God's power, strength, and mercy. And that is exactly what Christ offers.

Of all things I have learned, one thing I never tire of sharing is this: Grief is a legitimate emotion, a celebration of a loss. A loss worthy of rejoicing. A loss born of love, want, and hope.

For years I believed that if I was grieving, I was not faithful. This is a lie. We should grieve as we love…passionately.

Fearlessly.

Joyfully.

Relentlessly.

With anticipation, want, and need.

Dare anyone to tell you, "Chin up" or "Let's do this at home," look them square in the eye, and say, "Jesus wept."

We grieve beings we loved beyond our understanding. But our hurt isn't the end of the story. Our grief is at the foot of the cross. It is where we celebrate loving well and mourn those we've lost. It is where we crawl into the lap of a Father who loves and conquered the world. A loving and good Father paid the ultimate price for a perfect ending.

I think often of Barb—of her strength and compassion as she nursed her son in his final days, and how she still nurses the children of other mothers. Where does that kind of strength come from? Often, I suspect it is in the surrender. In the broken spaces, where we acknowledge He alone is our comfort.

It is no small thing to love so greatly, knowing full well that love can lead to the deepest place of loss and grief. Let us not waste a single moment ignoring life by fearing death, defying grief, or mistrusting a dear and precious God who waits patiently, loves perfectly, and restores wholly.

Of course
the work is
impossible,
but you are
a mother.
Impossible is
your middle
name.

Chapter 8

ONCE UPON A TIME...

I am about to do something new. See, I
have already begun! Do you not see it? I will
make a pathway through the wilderness. I
will create rivers in the dry wasteland.

ISAIAH 43:19

In a span of five years, we were bombarded by loss, illness, and grief. Justin's niece died. Both of his sisters had breast cancer; so did his mom. His dad died of West Nile virus. And then, Justin's brother died. At the time, I wished I had some kind of special prayer that would make God ease up on us.

The morning Justin's brother, Josh, was killed in a car accident was one of the most traumatic days of our lives. He was Justin's business partner. We owned the ranch together. We socialized with him and his wife. Our lives were entirely intertwined. And he, at age 48, was our 11-year-old John's best friend. They were inseparable. From the moment Josh got off work and John was released from his studies, they wandered the ranch, hunted hogs, tracked deer, and chased snakes.

On that dreadful morning, I sat on the front porch of Josh's house and listened to the devastation leaking from inside.

My dear friend Marcy's van approached around the drive, and as it appeared from behind a clump of cedar trees, I ran toward her. Marcy was a godly woman who knew her Bible inside and out. Maybe she would be able to explain the secret to surviving this much hurt. And more importantly, maybe she could help save my children from the "Amerine curse."

She threw the minivan into park and jumped from the vehicle, and I fell into her arms.

"Marcy, how do I save my children? This family is cursed! Everyone keeps dying! How can I save them?"

Marcy was stern. "You can't believe that, Jami! You are not cursed. Your children are not cursed. You have to believe that isn't true."

I wanted to. I wanted to believe that wasn't true. I wanted to believe that we were loved and protected by a kind and loving God. But I believed more in the idea that there was a code, some hidden scroll that ensured long life, health, and happiness.

I wanted this to be true too, and I wanted a copy of the methodology to stop anything bad from happening. I wanted to be chosen, protected, and adored by my Father in heaven.

People of Joy

Our season of heartache and loss finally came to a head months later when we faced the longest day of our lives. We had been involved in a treacherous lawsuit, and on this day, in the mediation room of a lawyer's office, my husband, Justin, and I spent 13 hours fighting for our livelihood. We feared we would lose everything. Our four children—Maggie, John, Luke, and Sophie—along with my mother-in-law, Iris, and other family and friends, had held vigil, praying for God to save us. He did. We were triumphant that day, and we slept oh-so-peacefully that night for the first time in a year.

Half-conscious as I awakened the next morning at an uncharacteristically late hour, I noticed Justin was already gone for the day; I had slept through his departure. As I stretched and yawned, becoming more cognizant, I realized I had experienced a very vivid dream during the night. In the dream, a little girl was in bed beside me; I looked at her and said, "Good morning, Allison!" She smiled brightly and responded, "Good morning, Mommy!"

Well, we don't have a little girl named Allison. I lay there thinking back on all we'd faced in recent months, all the kids had suffered. My poor, precious Justin was exhausted and almost broken from the weight of this year's experiences, but this day was finally different. We were at a crossroads; we had fought for truth, and we had won. I think when you fight long and hard for something, and then that struggle ends, sometimes you aren't quite sure what to do next.

But I was sure. God filled my heart with the "what's next," and it was pure poetry.

I grabbed my phone off the nightstand and hit Justin's name on my contact list.

"Good morning!" he answered. "How did you sleep?"

"Like the dead!"

Laughter. "Me too! What do you have going on today?"

"I need to tell you something," I said abruptly.

Justin hesitated. "Um. Okay?"

The words flew from my sleepy throat. "Justin, I had a dream about a little girl. I know you're going to think I'm crazy, but I have to tell you anyway. We're starting a new chapter in our lives; I want to rewrite our story. I want the kids to see that in the midst of terror we were true to our faith, and our God was faithful to us. I want the kids to witness what it means to walk in blind faith, not just when we are in trouble, but when we're climbing up out of the mud and mire. I want them to know that we will continue to be the people we claim to be, no matter what. I do not want to be 'the poor Amerines.' I want to be people of immense joy. Justin, I want to adopt a child!"

Dead silence.

And then, in his deepest, most dangerous "business-speak" voice, he said, "I'll call you back."

Click.

Hmm. That wasn't very joyful. I had overstepped. This brilliant man of mine had just fought the battle of a lifetime and succeeded. And here I was, less than ten hours later, nagging him to make a life-altering change. *You're awesome, Jami. Wife of the year goes to…someone else.*

I started pacing the floor. As I hoped he would call back, I thought of ways to explain myself and save our marriage. I would tell him I must have been asleep if I said that; I didn't know what he was talking about. Yes, I would pretend it was sleep talk! We would move on from there.

And then the theme song from *Superman* blared from my iPhone, and that meant my beloved Justin was calling. With a dry mouth, I cleared my throat and began the dialogue for "take two" of Act I: "Good morning, Justin! How did you sleep?"

Silence.

"Justin?"

"Jami."

"Justin, I am so sorry. I didn't mean it; I just…"

"Jami, you may look into this. On my end, I'll make a call to the lawyer. I have to call him anyway to tie up some loose ends. You need to understand that, per our experience, it could take weeks for him to call me back. I will ask him about what agency we should use. That's it. I have a company to rebuild; I understand what you're saying, but this cannot be all-consuming for me right now. I will let you know *if* I hear back from him. Okay?"

"Okay."

I sat on the bed in silence. The kids were all still asleep. My head was spinning. What was it I had said? "Rewrite our story"? "Be people of joy"? Maybe I was just a busybody, afraid that the drama being over would bring me immense boredom.

Then my phone rang. Was Superman calling back already? "Hello?"

"Christian Homes," he blurted.

I stammered, "You reached the lawyer already?"

"Jami, *he* answered the phone. His secretary is on maternity leave, and get this...she and her husband picked up their newborn adopted son on Monday from Christian Homes. He said we should use Christian Homes."

And so it began.

A New Chapter

Looking back on my initial thought process about adoption, I believe I was being truthful. I did want a new hope, a new joy. But I also had a habit of throwing virgins into the volcano. (Metaphorically speaking, of course. We don't live near a volcano.) I thought the right sacrifice might provide the right outcome. After so much tragedy, I actually believed if I worked harder, I would be spared more hurt.

Save orphans? Well, then I would get to be a mom in a new way and pacify a God who seemed to have cursed my family. Marinated in grief and confusion about the will of God, I was certain this time I would placate the God of Israel as I methodically filled out forms to save the least of these.

I dove right into the adoption process like nothing I had ever done before. I filled out paperwork and gathered documents, and we prayed for "Allison" or whomever it was God had in mind for us. We shared what we were doing with family members. Some were excited; others were confused. I would explain, "There is plenty of room in this family and a significant capacity to love. We want to share." Miracles happened—like openings in training seminars—when, otherwise, we would have been set back months in our certification. And then it was time for our final home visit and interview. This was it; after this, all we had to do was wait for a child in need.

The kids were clean. The house was spotless. Coffee was brewing, and banana bread was baking. The hills were alive with the sound of perfection when Miss Cynthia, our social worker, knocked at the door.

First, she looked around the house, and then she spoke alone with Justin and me. It was a lovely visit. Then she wanted to meet the children: Maggie, 16; John, 13; Luke, 12; and Sophie, 9. They were polite and funny. We were relieved. That is, until Miss Cynthia said the most bone-chilling words I had ever heard: "May I speak to each of the children alone?"

I looked at Justin.

Justin looked at me.

I wish I had a picture of our faces. Alone? Away from us?

Maggie, John, and Sophie could surely be trusted, but Luke? We laughed nervously. "Why, of course you may." As the social worker escorted Maggie to the playroom, we looked across the table at our youngest son. Without missing a beat, we started in.

Justin: "Luke, son, please—this is *not* a comedy sketch."

Me: "Luke, I know that I *do* raise my voice, and I *do* threaten you on occasion, but I never have actually carried out those threats, and if I did you probably would have survived."

Justin: "Jami, stop talking! Luke, son, we love you, and we really feel a calling to adopt another child. It would be great if you could, uh, well…"

Miss Cynthia: "Okay, who's next?"

Luke, never taking his huge green eyes from our faces, stood his lanky self up, flashed those wicked dimples, and said, "I'll go next!"

They were gone 30 minutes, and we could hear Cynthia's belly laughs the whole time. I was pacing, and Justin sat on the edge of the couch, face in his hands. When Cynthia and Luke emerged from the playroom, Cynthia was grinning from ear to ear and wiping tears from her eyes. "Who's next?"

Well, at least the interviews were going to continue. To this day, Luke will not tell the secrets he revealed, but at least Miss Cynthia didn't run screaming from the house. And we were certified to adopt.

If nothing else ever comes of this book, let it be said here and now: Adoption is beautiful. It is straight from Jesus. Nine months to the day of my initial phone call to Justin, Cynthia called us and said we needed to come to her office, because they had a placement to discuss with us. On the drive over, I knew we were going to hear about our new baby. In my heart, I knew it was a baby boy.

Sure enough, the picture on Cynthia's computer screen showed a newborn Hispanic boy. He had a cleft chin and a full head of the blackest hair I had ever seen. It wasn't until the next day, when I held him for the first time, that I realized I had not seen "blackest" until I saw his eyes. They were gorgeous. He was beautiful, he was perfect, and he was instantly one of us.

During our nine-month wait, we had collected little mementos of our adoption journey on a shelf in the living room. One of the items was a little blue cross with the words, "For this child, I prayed. 1 Samuel 1:27." And so it came to be that our little boy was named Samuel, after the scripture reference, and Michael, in honor of my younger brother. We would call him "Sam." Yes…the Sam who would later launch "The Spill" and the perpetually sticky floors. Yes, the Sam who would become one of our keep-us-on-our-toes Vandals. I didn't know any of that then, of course. And it wouldn't have mattered a smidge. Because I was smitten.

As they placed the blue bundle in my arms, I said, "Hello, Sam. I'm your mommy."

Sam.

He is thoroughly Sam.

We served this little cherub with a newfound hope for the goodness that came from the darkness.

Risking a Broken Heart

I was stubbornly determined on no more hurt. I would serve the least of these on my terms. Sam was so much younger than Sophie, it only made sense to us that we add at least one or two more children to our lives. This time, we decided we would go the foster-to-adopt route. Before you champion my cause, know full well, I believed foster-to-adopt meant we would get a foster child, keep a foster child, adopt a foster child. Appease the pain gods and save the babies.

Our foster license came in the mail on a horrible afternoon when Justin had lost a huge bid for a job he desperately needed. I met him at the door, waving the paper. "Look what came in the mail! Maybe we will finally meet our baby!"

Justin growled at me like a guard dog behind a chain-link fence at a car impound. Yeah, that kind of growl. I slowly backed away and threw a macaroni casserole into his cage.

He didn't understand the hard work of world saving.

"Don't worry!" I hummed. "They won't call today, silly."

It was 10:09 that night when my phone lit up on my nightstand. Justin snored next to me, and I squinted to make out the words "Christian Homes" on the screen. In my mind, I saw a huge Doberman pinscher with a spiked collar jumping over a fence, tearing apart my jugular, and gnawing on my spleen.

I snuck into the closet, so Justin wouldn't kill me.

"Hello?" I whispered.

"Hello, Jami. It's Angelica from Christian Homes."

"Yes, hello, what's wrong?"

Angelica explained, "We have a placement request. A baby boy. He's at the hospital near your home. The only information I have is that he's injured."

I probed further. "Is he adoptable?"

She paused, and then said, "I don't know, Jami, but he's only three months old, and he's injured and all alone. Do you want to go sit with him until we know more? Or should I call someone else?"

People say they can't do foster care because they are afraid they'll get hurt.

"No," I whispered. "I'm so sorry. Justin is asleep, and I don't think I can."

In my mind, I pretty much said it to an injured baby boy. I am sorry for your problems, but I can't help you. I am afraid I'll get hurt.

"Okay," she said. "Please pray we find someone quickly."

"Absolutely. Sorry." I hung up and was startled to find Justin standing behind me.

"Who was that?"

I jumped, still alert to the fact I could be instantly mauled to death. "Sorry, I didn't know you were awake. It was a foster placement request."

"And?"

"I told them no."

"Why?"

"Well...It was a baby boy. He's at the hospital alone, and he's injured."

"Do you want me to go?"

"No, I told them you were asleep. I...I thought it wasn't a good time?"

He was incredulous. "Are we going to help a child in need or not?"

Not if we could get hurt, right? I thought.

"Jami?" he asked, bringing me back to the moment. "Call her back. One of us needs to go."

I nervously dialed, and Angelica answered on the first ring. "Angelica, this is Jami Amerine. I can be there in 15 minutes." The minute I hung up, I knew it was worth risking a broken heart for a scared, broken boy.

Ridiculously tiny, terribly injured, with a big blond head, we would fondly nickname him "Charlie."

I Can

I was asked for my ID at the nurses' station. They directed me to a room that was dark but for the beeping monitors and a soft white night-light glowing from behind the bed. The impossibly small boy was hooked up to oxygen, an IV drip, and heart monitors. A lump formed in my throat.

"I can't," I whispered.

The nurse appeared behind me in the doorway. I knew her instantly. It was Barb, the mother of Brock, the young boy who died of brain cancer. She was naturally beautiful and artistically "cool." Everything I wished to be…except a mom who had lost her boy. My mind stirred up images of his little coffin and thoughts of the injustice of his death, along with questions of how that could happen and how they survived such tragedy.

"Hey!" she chirped. "Are you from the foster agency?"

"Yes."

Her eyebrows knit together. "Don't I know you?" she asked.

"Yes, I'm Jami. My daughter was…is… the same age as your Brock."

"Oh, yeah! How are you?"

How am I? How am I? Let's see… I am a wreck. How are you here, working as a pediatric nurse, and not in a rubber room somewhere?

"I'm okay. How are you?" I answered softly.

"I'm in love with this little guy." She motioned to the bed. "Come meet him. I just called my husband and told him I was sneaking him out in my lunch box." She laughed. Her laugh was fragrant and genuine. Tears burned my eyes.

She was a survivor of the ultimate loss. If she could, I could.

"He's hurt, but he needs some cuddles. Can you climb onto the bed, and I'll hand him to you?"

Barb, with an addictive smile and hippie-chick swagger—a woman who had birthed and buried, loved and lost—asked if I was willing and able. *Can you? Can I?*

"Yes, I can."

I climbed onto the bed, and Barb handed me my first foster placement. His eyes fluttered open, and he looked at me most quizzically. I settled back and introduced myself as best I knew how. "Hello, friend. My name is Jami, with no *e*." Then, I read to him all night. He never took his eyes off me, which was either the Holy Spirit or the morphine drip. But it was there I learned what my heart was capable of. It was there I first saw how my imperfections and weaknesses were comprised of that which I did not understand.

On that day in the hospital, I'm not sure what Charlie saw as he stared at me. But I saw something in this baby boy, an air of nobility, and I fell fearlessly and hopelessly in love.

Through Christ

I recall during our first adoption journey, when our caseworker, Cynthia, came out for our intake interview, the only thing I checked as a "no can do" was seizures. She asked me about it. I explained, "I can't do seizures because they terrify me. I can handle anything but seizures."

Of course, when adopting a newborn, there is no medical evidence they are seizure-free, but Sam's birth mother made no indication that seizures would be an issue.

He had his first febrile seizure when he was 10 months old. He had his second when he was 15 months old. Since then, he's had about four more. They only happen when he has a high fever. They are terrifying. And it turns out, I *can*. I can handle seizures, because this little boy needs me to.

I can do anything in my power to comfort him and keep him safe until they subside. I hate seizures, but I cannot possibly hate them more than Sam does. After he's had one, he is disoriented and scared. He weeps silently, a fatigued cry, and craves my embrace.

I can do that.

It is my pleasure.

I can pray, and I can provide this angel with whatever is humanly possible for me to give until he has his sea legs.

I'm convinced that a mom who trusts Christ can do things no other human can.

Suddenly, you bravely unscrew the top of that sippy cup that had been festering under the seat of your minivan in 100-degree temperatures. The pressure that has accumulated under suction burps and sizzles as you take off the lid. You dump the black, moldy plasma out—you suspect it may have been milk—and it thumps into the bottom of your stainless-steel sink. The mass starts to slither away from the drain; you pause to gag and quickly turn on the hot water. You shove your fake French-manicured fingernail into the top of the rubber stopper and sling the stopper into the scalding stream of water. To ensure the thing dies and the cup is safe, you dump a gallon of bleach into the sink. Bile rises in your throat, *but the cup won't win*. You even blow air through the stopper to make sure it is clear of any more pungent filth. There are seasoned plumbers who would shudder in your presence.

You can, and you did. Of course the work is impossible, but you are a mother. *Impossible* is your middle name.

Part 2

REWARD
AND RECEIVE

Faith, in the sense in which I am here using the word,
is the art of holding on to things your reason has
once accepted, in spite of your changing moods.

C.S. LEWIS, *MERE CHRISTIANITY*

Unless I am laid out flat on my back, when is there time for an epiphany?

Chapter 9

NIGHT NIGHT

Come to me, all of you who are weary and
carry heavy burdens, and I will give you rest.

MATTHEW 11:28

I was supposed to read an article for one of the man-babies' college requirements, and halfway through I realized I had no idea what I was reading. I had, in fact, redecorated the master bathroom in my mind.

The routine I counted toward my worthiness looked perfect. I'd get up at 4:30 a.m., Bible in one hand, coffee in the other. The goal was to be still and sit with Jesus. We would talk about the kids, the new foster baby, Justin and me, my finances, and how grateful I am for this life, and...wait. What the heck? Is that a spider on the mantel? That's too big to be a spider... Oh my gosh, it's a feral cat! How did that get in the house? What if it has rabies? Wait, that is not a cat; that's a stuffed Batman. Good grief, I'll just put that away so it won't distract me. Well, heavens to Betsy, did a dust storm come through here? I can't sit with Jesus until I dust the mantel.

Before I know it, it's 7:15. The entire house is spotless, and my Bible and now-cold coffee sit untouched. I cleaned out the fridge, packed lunches, organized the toy box, and ordered this nifty air cleaner for the room to keep the mantel from getting dusty, so I can spend tomorrow morning with Jesus. Squirrel!

Activities I meant to do, believing they would deepen my joy and intensify my walk with Jesus…I missed them. But I am not wicked. I did things to maintain my home, the sacred ground, and my family, whom I dearly love. Didn't that Proverbs supermom do that? Up early, rocking a booth at the Christmas in November bazaar with trinkets she made? Baking bread, taking the kids to school? Against these things, there is no law. Wait, wrong scripture. Let me just look up that verse here on my phone, after I check Facebook… Oh! Look at that; Liz had her baby. So sweet. I need to get on Amazon and order her something…

I get a billion things done in a day. I am a one-woman marvel. But do I really get *to* Jesus? Rarely. And honestly, for years, I did not know exactly how to reconcile this. As much as I wanted to, my brain didn't stop unless forced to do so. I was required to ask myself, "Will a stomach bug be my only reprieve?" I would add this to my list of prayers: "Jesus, help me. Help me be focused. Help me to give You some time. Help me seek Your presence without distraction. I pray these things in Jesus's name. Amen."

This prayer, a prayer I have found a hundred times in old journals, was the wrong prayer. I was missing the fact that God knows how distractible I have been and continue to be. I believe He has always known He would meet me in the chaos rather than if or when I became more focused and had fewer neuroses.

Don't get me wrong; I remain intrigued by a simpler way of life. Sometimes I wonder about what life and parenting would be like if I lived in a grass hut. If a missionary walked by and told me about the saving love of Jesus Christ, would I be saved? If he left no Bible, highlighters, study guides, or spiral notebooks, would the knowledge he gave me, the truth of Jesus Christ, be enough to leave me redeemed? And what about my kids? Would I pass that truth along in its pure form? Would they be saved? Would they be cursed by my madness? Am I cursed by my parents' madness, and they by theirs?

Where do my kids stop and I start?

And I've forced myself to consider, was I even a factor in their saving faith?

In this life, in a house and not that theoretical hut, I was still betting I was responsible. I had to do whatever I could to make myself produce fruit and force the children to commit to Jesus so that they, too, would produce this fruit.

The work was impossible.

Of all the lies I believed in the earlier years of parenting, the greatest was that my hard work could bring me peace.

So I worked. I was depressed and chubby. I never rested, and I never found relief or assurance. In that buffet-line faith of a little taste of Moses, a tiny dose of Jesus, I was hoarding and feasting on all the law-entrenched entrées I could get my anxious hands on. I was entirely obsessed with my sin. And most of the time, my indiscretions were not "sins" at all, like missing church because I was pregnant and vomiting; going over my Weight Watchers points allowance; or sleeping too late because I'd been up all night praying, and then not waking on time to…pray.

My snowballing fear kept me from rest. In the middle of my hard work, I could not understand why I was incapable of producing the fruit of the Spirit—primarily peace and self-control. But an apple tree doesn't try to produce apples; it just does. I was trying to make fruit happen instead of seeing it naturally manifested through a life connected to the true vine.

Forced Stillness

As any of my children will testify, I refuse to give Satan too much credit, except in incidents of stomach flu, stomach viruses, and food poisoning. The stomach flu is my kryptonite. The interruption of life as we know it, everything we hold dear, comes completely unraveled with that little whimper, "Mommy, my stomach hurts." And with that whimper, a symphony of agony and laundry bursts forth. The domino effect is painfully slow; one by one, night after night, they fall. And heaven help everyone if Mom gets it.

(Allow me to step up on my soapbox. For the love of all that is good, sick people, stay home! You are not needed in society until you are done vomiting. There will be other science fairs, another birthday party, and a dozen other school assemblies, I promise.)

It had been a couple years since our last exposure to the bug, but alas, it hit. Stumbling through the dark, grabbing buckets, and strategically spreading towels, we were on high alert.

In the wee hours, I couldn't fight the urge any longer. As I clung to the toilet and heaved my last, I began to weep at the anarchy that would inevitably ensue. Days of missed school, evenings of makeup homework, and towels, pajamas, and sheets stacked outside the laundry room door. That smell in the spot you'd thought for sure you cleaned up. The pain of the first day back at the gym, the water retention from the tiny sips of Gatorade—everything would be a process of climbing out of the pit. It would be weeks before we would attain normalcy. I crawled back to bed, shivering and dripping sweat.

My husband does not get sick. We have been married 25 years. I think he has been sick maybe twice, and one of those times was when he had his wisdom teeth pulled. While I do not understand how this is possible, especially when this man literally has had as many as four different children's bodily fluids spewed on him at once, I thank God for his superhuman immunity.

At that point in my near-death experience, as I lay in bed, Justin tossed an extra blanket over me and asked, "What can I do for you?"

"Please kill me," I said.

He refused, and I mumbled my disdain for his cowardice as he left me to suffer. I heard him tending to Sam down the hall. In the nursery, our infant foster son began to fuss. I heard Justin enter the room to console him, and then I listened to another child start to blow chunks. *Cringe.*

"Justin, bring the baby to me." Imagine my martyr tone here.

"No, you're sick."

"It's okay. Just lay him with me and go help the other victims."

Justin placed the baby next to me on the bed. For the record, you're not allowed to have a foster baby in the bed with you while you sleep. However, since I wasn't sleeping but was, in fact, dying, I broke no rules. My sense of smell was in overdrive. Nausea swirled, and I squeezed my eyes shut to stop the room from spinning. As I rested my cheek on top of this baby's precious head, he snuggled into me and reached up to tug at my hair. He cooed, I shushed him, and he giggled. His creamy skin was softer and warmer than anything I remember. He squirmed a bit, and I breathed in his perfect baby smell and gagged just a little.

This moment is forever among my favorite memories—even the stomach flu part. When do I ever stop? Unless I am laid out flat on my back, when is there time for an epiphany? Such moments with this precious child of God were so few and far between. I am so busy. As much as this little boy needed me, I needed him that much more. I played with his toes, patted his diapered bum, rubbed his cool ears, and listened to his natural breath. His little thighs were like butter, and his innocence flooded me with immense peace. I was utterly broken, flat on my back, and finally experiencing God's peace.

Rest. You should rest. Whatever. But the truth is, just as grief is a vehicle by which we know and love God, a vessel by which we are healed, so, too, is rest. In the quiet (even though likely never a solid eight hours), in our drowsy states, we are most keen to the small, still voice I fully believe is God. Rest—an event moms chase after like a dog after a cat. Yet once we pounce, it is hardly the delicacy we imagined. True rest has only been afforded me when I've stopped trying to create peace and instead let it wash over me.

If I thought foster care was the key to a peaceable existence, I was wrong on a hundred different levels. However, aside from the hard work of caring for an injured infant and tending to his physical therapy appointments, parent visits, and other needs, he wasn't the issue.

Luke was.

Pastor Luke

I loved my boys as teens. I loved sporting events, their humor, and their ridiculousness. John and Luke kept us in stitches. They were constantly "on." And whether they were beating each other to a pulp or roasting a turkey at 1:00 in the morning for a snack, I loved being their mom.

Friends called our younger son "Pastor Luke." He was everyone's hero and best friend. In any given week, he'd mention a parade of new pals.

"Can I go to David's?"

"Who is David?"

"My best friend."

"Can I go to Parker's?"

"Who?"

"My best friend."

"Wait, who stole and totaled the car?"

"Tate, my best friend."

The month after Charlie was placed with us, Luke went on a mission trip to inner-city Houston to relocate homeless people from under a condemned bridge. I went to pick him up at the end of the session. He met me at the car, and I had never seen him so happy.

"I want to introduce you to my new best friend! He lives under that tree. His name is Crazy Mike. He doesn't wear any pants or underwear. Just don't look down."

This is Luke, looking out for the little guy and those in need. He loves everyone and has no enemies. But upon returning home from that camp, things began to deteriorate. He was increasingly depressed, and he was rebellious like nothing we had experienced before. Intermittently, he was himself, horsing around with John, swimming with Sam and Charlie, and lying in the girls' room, listening to music.

One afternoon, we had an injured respite-care infant in our home. There are times when other foster parents need a break for medical reasons or travel plans, and other families provide respite. I was happy to have this little one close to my body in a baby wrap as I started preparing dinner in the kitchen. Sam and Charlie were napping.

All was rather peaceful.

Until I heard John's booming voice asking, "Hey, Luke, do you think I can do a handstand on the banister?"

Chills ran up my spine. Gingerly but swiftly, I unhooked the sling that kept the tiny baby strapped to me, so I could stop the madness that was about to go down. I could hear Luke's response.

"Of course you can! What makes you think you can't do a handstand on the banister? You are very physically fit."

I placed the baby in the bassinet in the breakfast nook and took off down the hall.

John agreed, "You're right, Luke. Thanks, man."

"Anytime."

I was too late. All the effects of a 6-foot-3, 185-pound man-baby failing at a handstand on the banister ensued.

Sheetrock fell, along with John, the banister, and the chandelier. The beauty and folly of manbabies—John survived. We cleaned up the mess and laughed and loved through it all. It is among my favorite memories. This was my life, this was my family. Chaos and lunacy.

Broken

When it rains, it pours and then pours some more. During this monsoon season of foster care stress and worry about Luke, I became ill and ended up in the hospital for nine days. To this wiped and worried mama, the time to lie dormant was a relief. Yes, they wake you up to check your blood pressure and take your temperature. But let's face it: If I were at home, someone would have woken me up anyway. And they wouldn't do it to see if I was alive; they'd do it to ask me for something. Say, a bottle, or a diaper change, or my credit card for a pizza, or bail money. Or someone would nudge me to ask, "Are we seriously out of Colby-Jack cheese?"

If someone wakes me up at the hospital, it is for my well-being. And then I can ask them to please bring me cranberry juice over ice.

So this hospital stay was a welcome reprieve. It was a restful time, a forced leave of absence, if you will. Granted, I was very sick, but in that sickness, I was better off in the hospital. I was better cared for. I was wheeled to MRIs and CT scans. I was given painkillers and fluids.

Turns out that good things can happen when we're weak. In my broken state, in a hospital room on the fourth floor, the troops at home rallied and took care of things while I rested. Justin was probably relieved I was not lying on the closet floor, having a meltdown again.

But the mama guilt was getting to me. Even though things at home were going well, I wanted to know if this was okay. Or even better than okay; maybe it was holy! I remember turning to the book of 2 Corinthians in the hospital, meditating on God's sweet promise:

"My grace is all you need. My power works best in weakness." So now I am glad to boast about my weaknesses, so that the power of Christ can work through me (2 Corinthians 12:9).

In that brokenness, alone for the first time in ages, I loved knowing Jesus was still Jesus when I couldn't walk to the bathroom by myself. More importantly, I felt safe knowing Jesus is supercharged when I am an utter disaster. That's one awesome Jesus, because I am a disaster like 99 percent of the time.

Peace Isn't Just for the Perfect

Weeks after my release, I was staying in a hotel while traveling for speaking engagements. We had seven children at the time, and while it was hard to be away from them, I felt the grace of having a night to myself. I fell asleep in the early evening, totally exhausted.

When I woke, I struggled to recognize my surroundings. I got up, made a pot of coffee, pulled on my cozy robe, and opened the light-blocking drapes. I was pleased to see the sun wasn't up yet. I smiled to myself as I opened up my laptop. I would have an entire day to work alone in the hotel, and I was eager to get started.

That was when I saw the time. It was only 12:15 a.m. I had been asleep less than four hours. At home, four hours of uninterrupted sleep would be a miracle. Between the teens texting me to ask me if I am awake, the toddlers requiring comfort after a nightmare, and the baby demanding a bottle, I rarely get uninterrupted sleep.

I turned off the coffeepot, closed the drapes, and climbed back into the crispy hotel-grade Egyptian cotton sheets.

It was both a relief...and a burden.

I lay there, giggling to myself. And then I worried about my husband, home alone with our brood. He was probably exhausted. I felt dejected I wasn't there to help him. Unable to fall back to sleep,

I got up and worked until 5:00, fell asleep on my keyboard, and was startled awake at 7:20 when the neighbor in the adjoining room started his shower.

I felt all the pangs of a protracted night, and my keyboard was firmly imprinted on my left cheek. I dragged my weary body to the shower and stretched the kinks out of my neck and back. Steam chased me from the bathroom, and I poured a cup of coffee into a sorry little Styrofoam cup and added powdered creamer. I stared out the window at the unfamiliar town, straining to spy a Starbucks on the horizon.

And I bemoaned the day before me.

The sun poured forth the freshness of a new day, yet I felt less than fresh. Scripture floated into my mind: *Come to me, all of you who are weary…and I will give you rest* (Matthew 11:28). Yet in spite of the rest He offers me, I sleep on my keyboard and then bathe in culpability when I put up my feet to take a break. Rest brings guilt; it buys condemnation. I associated rest with something shameful rather than a blessing. Furthermore, I associated rest with lost control. I believed that if I stopped, everything would come crumbling down around me.

It's curious how the Maker of heaven and earth produced this body for survival in an unconscious state. Eyes closed, breath steady, mind in a playland of nonsense. Occasionally, darkness creeps in and a chase ensues, or great terrors play out. Still, this is the slumber He fashioned for me.

Society demands I work harder, invest more, and rest less. God waits for me. The blessing of rest waits in His gentle hands, but instead of curling up in His majestic creation of sleep, I analyze, supervise, and contrive.

I am weary. And I am most weary of the weariness. I am worn out from self-induced standards of efficiency and the bragging rights of minimal repose. When did "I only got five hours of sleep" become something to boast about?

If I stood before my Lord, and He presented me with a lovely package—a box wrapped in shiny paper, with an enormous glittery bow—would I decline the offering? Would I boastfully retort, "I don't need that from you"?

Of course not. Yet He offers me rest, and I refuse the gift often.

But not that day in the hotel room. The thought of that gift and His peace won the battle for my thoughts. I closed the heavy curtains once again. I changed back into pajamas. I hung the "Do Not Disturb" sign on the outside doorknob, and I chose to rest.

A gift.

Whether rest looks like coffee with a friend, bubble baths, or a moment alone on the closet floor, begging for His help maneuvering homework and dinner, it's a reminder that God cares for the weary.

Real rest is the rest of belief. Not simply believing God exists, but believing God is alive and present in my life. Believing He knows me and fashioned me a certain way, and I am His beloved daughter. Rest comes with believing He is in charge. He knows me, my kids, Justin, and my heart. And for this sweet, brief day, I banished the voice saying, "Peace that passes understanding is just for the women who work hard enough to earn it."

I accepted the gift. I pulled the covers to my chin and sighed with gratitude and relief. I knew God had me in His care.

What I didn't know was that as I let go of perfection that day, God was preparing me to let go of my son.

Let Jesus be Jesus. He will not leave or forsake your kids, no matter what.

Chapter 10

SECRET SAUCE

The Holy Spirit helps us in our weakness. For
example, we don't know what God wants us to
pray for. But the Holy Spirit prays for us with
groanings that cannot be expressed in words.

ROMANS 8:26

At 1:26 in the morning, Justin's phone rang. We sat bolt upright in bed.

"This is Justin Amerine." He listened for a moment and then responded, "Yes, he is my son. Is he okay?"

My heart stopped.

"Yes, okay. Thank you. I'll be right there."

He hung up and got out of bed. I couldn't bring myself to ask. But Justin answered the question anyway.

"It's Luke. The police have him. He's alive...*until I get there.*"

Pass the Secret Sauce, Please

Control—the opposite of parenting. Some families *seem* absolutely perfect: The street-corner yards are manicured, the cars are all cleaned and waxed, and everything has the appearance of controlled perfection. But what seems flawless isn't always that way.

A few months ago, I drove through an affluent neighborhood near Dallas, Texas, on my way to a speaking engagement. It was a sea of slate roofs. As I drove by, I saw a beautiful woman standing in a yard, screaming at a man in a navy-blue suit with a purple tie. He yelled back at her as he climbed into a black Mercedes. A woman on a cell phone power walked down the street, two baby boys snoozing in her jogging stroller. A few blocks down, an elderly couple sat on their porch, drinking from steaming mugs and reading the paper. As I turned into the church parking lot, I noticed two women embracing; one was crying.

Brokenness, excellence, blessings, and curses.

That neighborhood embodied, from the outside, everything I used to want. But real life gets in the way. Childhood cancer, husbands with porn addictions, job losses, parents with Alzheimer's, fires, drunk drivers, economic downturns, teen pregnancy, learning disabilities. No matter how manicured your lawn, you can't cut out the risk.

I just wanted to be able to make things *perfect*. If everything were in order and I did things impeccably, then my kids would be happy and healthy, my marriage would be better, and I would have firm thighs and toned abs.

But striving didn't change the results. And there was no ignoring it…our son was spiraling out of control.

Phone calls from the police became the norm. We were at our wits' end. No matter what we did, we couldn't keep Luke in the house. He slept on the second floor; I slept on the floor outside his door. Still, in the middle of the night we would get a call that made our hearts race. The voice on the other end would say, "Hey, Mrs. Amerine, could you come get Luke?"

Letting Go

Justin and I started to take turns sleeping on the couch and picking up Luke from the police station. This was not going to get better.

I was a one-woman circus of hypocrisy, praised for my efforts in foster care and tell-it-like-it-is blog posts, whispered about behind my back because of my wayward son. Finally, with Luke's illegal activity threatening our foster license, and being down to the wire with Charlie's final placement, out of energy and answers, we sat down with Luke as a family. We decided to relinquish our foster care license and turn Charlie over to our provider after spending a year in our care.

Our explanation was not a threat. It was an act of mercy and love. The goal was to offer Luke all we had. We got into foster care as a family, and we would get out as a family. Luke's search for whatever he was searching for could cost us Charlie's placement. If we made the choice before it came to this, we eliminated the chance of Charlie being removed from our home *because of Luke.* We knew that such a result would drive a wedge between him and his siblings, and that wasn't what we wanted for Charlie or Luke.

Luke was beside himself. He promised he would never sneak out again. He was done. He would protect Charlie at all costs. We hugged and wept.

At 3:00 that morning the police called. Justin went and got Luke. The situation was much more horrific than we had suspected. We knew it was time to let go—not of Charlie, but of Luke.

The next morning, Justin, Luke, and I left and drove 500 miles to the Marine Military Academy in Harlingen, Texas. We made arrangements by phone to borrow $30,000 to pay for the school. Luke never spoke. I never stopped sobbing.

Everything I believed about my ability as a mother, every truth I knew about my son, was slipping through my fingers. Word spread quickly; friends and family were calling and messaging. I barely knew how to respond or explain. We would do anything to save this boy—from himself.

The marines told us to say our goodbyes. Luke looked straight ahead. His disdain for us oozed like dishwashing suds from the broken dishwasher we used to have.

In some random hotel room in San Antonio, Justin and I sat in tacky upholstered chairs with cacti embroidered all over them. We wept and recounted our errors. We suffered fiercely, hopelessly, helplessly, and the tears fell uncontrollably. Whether we knew it then or not, they fell onto sacred ground.

My Child Would Never

Here is a list of stuff I can't handle:

I can't do seizures.

I can't be in the hospital for nine days.

I can't sew. Don't ask me.

I can't sing—it's truly a spectacle.

I can't stop eating Cheez-Its.

I can't…

I say the words, "I can't," and the universe gladly accepts the challenge. It's just like the word *never*. As in, *I would never send my child to military school* or *My child would never…*

Yeah, he sure might.

Here's a warning: If you say, "My child would never," they will do the very thing you said they would not do. Even if you say this while you're pregnant, before your child is even born, the bad juju cannot be filtered by the placenta.

My first encounter with this phenomenon—and yes, there

have been many, because I am a slow learner—happened with Luke. I was about seven months pregnant with him when a friend bemoaned her trial with her three-year-old daughter. The trial? The child refused to wear shoes. After leaving a potluck lunch at church, I said these words:

"Oh my word! Suzy is such a hick. 'Ainsley won't wear shoes.' Puh-lease! Just put shoes on the child. Who is in charge in this relationship?"

When I said these words, I imagine our unborn son's DNA, neurological makeup, and destiny were chemically altered. When I say Luke would not wear shoes as a child, I mean we had to put him in counseling because of his disdain for socks for six years. We placed him in horseback therapy to help him make some sort of cognitive brain connection, so he would not lose his ever-loving mind if we drove past a Payless. We had to go to marriage counseling because of the strain on our relationship from ongoing shoe battles. One time, we had to be escorted out of Sears by a mall cop because of an incident in Foot Locker. (We are still banned from all Foot Lockers in the western states and Kentucky, I think.) As he entered his teenage years, the situation continued to decline. He was six foot three at the ripe old age of fifteen. How do you make someone that size put on shoes?

You cannot.

We couldn't get him to comply. Of course, the issues went well beyond shoes. There was very little about his behavioral troubles that we could understand. And we couldn't connect with him. We had high hopes the marines could.

Consequences

This brings me to a difficult point in every parent's journey: discipline. I wish I could come to you and say, "This is how to properly discipline a child." But I don't know your child. All of our children have required different approaches. And we know them. The hardest part of sending Luke away to military school was conveying that our decision wasn't a punishment; it was a consequence. He struggled to understand that living in the moment could mean destroying his future. We had to make the hard choice, as unpleasant as it was, in order to save our hopes for his future.

At one point earlier in Luke's defiance, we had made an appointment with a counselor. Luke would not get in the car to go. He's two inches taller than my husband, and we were at a loss. A physical altercation seemed futile.

Almost instinctually, we started parenting Luke from a place of toddler logic. *These actions will result in this outcome.* We tell a child, "If you touch the stove, you will get burned." But we don't put a child's hand on the burner to teach them about a burn. And in the event they touch the burner, we don't sneer, "I told you so!" No, we address the issue. Hopefully, they will never do it again.

I think it is imperative to note three things when it comes to discipline.

1. Recognize That Legalism Produces Rebellion

How many jokes do you know about the preacher's daughter being a wild child? *Don't do this or else.* Of course, we need healthy boundaries, but when we focus too much on the rule itself, the real issue at hand becomes secondary. And if we offer no explanation as to the *why* of the rule, the forbidden becomes the obsession.

There are extremes. We knew of a homeschool family who allowed no television, radio, computers, or phones in their house—they were "devil boxes." When their oldest daughter turned 19, she left for Texas Tech. By the end of the first semester, she'd shaved her head and had a tattoo of "666" on the back of her neck. Her uncaged and immature character raged against an upbringing that couldn't be maintained in the world. I empathize with the parents' plight to maintain innocence in their home, but when you let someone out of the prison cell without preparation for life on the outside, their oppressed nature seeks indulgence.

A close friend's son is a great example. In general, Carson was beyond easy to raise. But when he was 13, he hit a rough patch. His interest in a girl led to a series of lies and a "sneaky" relationship. The consequence for lying to his parents was the loss of his phone.

In Luke's case, we told him, "You don't have to get in the car and go to counseling. It is up to you. You can choose to go with us. However, if you choose not to go and discuss these issues, we are no longer paying for your driver's education course."

2. Realize They Are Human

I recently met with a family whose 15-year-old son was caught looking at pornography. The family was crushed. Upon further investigation, they learned he was truly addicted to the activity. They provided their son with articles on child sex trafficking; they lectured him on the evils of pornography; and they took him to no fewer than six "healing retreats," where he was prayed over and purged of his nasty habit.

Here is the thing: A 15-year-old boy probably isn't going to be morally convicted by articles on sex trafficking. Healing retreats? Okay, well, you can lead a horse to water but…you know the rest. And yes, he did want to stop this activity, but he was motivated to stop only because he got caught and was then shamed. His penitence was a shame-based response. Immediately, he and his family began to focus on the sin. And when you talk about sin, what is the fifteen-year-old son focused on? That's right, naked ladies.

My advice to his parents was threefold:

1. Tell him he may not use your devices to watch pornography. You pay for those things, and you get to choose what is seen on them. Install filters and alerts to prevent him from viewing objectionable material.

2. Acknowledge that your child is a sexual being and has honest questions and curiosities. Tell him, "I understand about the curiosity, and I also understand desire. But I am concerned. I want to provide a safe place to discuss this, and while it is not what I want for you, I am here to help you as you mature in the process of making these choices. Choices I hope will be moral, ethical, and healthy."

3. Ask him how you can help him overcome his problem. Let him take an active part in his healing.

None of this is easy to convey to a boy who is thinking with his pituitary gland. But with these rules in place, continuing this behavior becomes riskier for him. He will have to look at porn in public locations. If he is caught, he will face the natural consequences of looking at inappropriate material at school or work. You are there to comfort and guide, but not to erase the issue and make it go away. It happened. Here's the music: face it.

At our core, we don't want to see our children hurting. And yes, when they get in trouble, it feels like a direct reflection on you as the parent. Believe me, I know. But when *we* sin, does God's character change, or is He accused of failing as our Father? Treating our children as individuals, capable of sin but fully perfected in Christ, is a game changer.

When Maggie was about seven she was an aspiring kleptomaniac. On three different occasions, she stole something from a friend's house. The first time, I knew she stole it. But I smuggled it back into the friend's backpack and then shamed Maggie privately. The second time, I did the same. The third time, she got caught red-handed. And the friend's mom called me and confronted me.

I made excuses. I covered for her. I was humiliated and ashamed.

And this is the real shame: Maggie should have returned the item and apologized. Instead, I took it personally, made up some ridiculous account of what I thought happened, and then systematically destroyed our relationship with that family. We moved to a different neighborhood. (I wish I were kidding.) I know, very mature. But the key element here is to recognize our children as apart from us and capable of sin. And because of Jesus, that sin is not the end of the world. Christ came to set us free from that destruction.

3. Remember Whose They Are

I would also like to address this question: "Well, what if my kid isn't saved?" So? Speak that over them. You can't make someone love Jesus. Go on, try. I did. And from the high horse of piety, you only bring more rebellion.

I have a close friend who has a child walking an impossible road. She doesn't bash her daughter over the head, but she confronts her with words like, "I disagree with these choices. I believe you will come to know and love Jesus. I am here to listen and lend advice where I can. I will not bail you out; I will not interfere with your natural consequences. But I love you, and I am praying for you."

Yes, she spends many a night awake, talking to God about these heartbreaking events. But no, there is very little else she can do. And frankly, I trust God as a parent way more than I trust me. He is up for these challenges. Ask Him how to discern the best path; after all, let us not forget they are His kids.

Let me say that again: *They are His kids.*

Take the terror out of the situation. The worst-case scenario is death. Guess what? He conquered that already. Discipline from a place of the Spirit. Our punishment is over and done. We are wholly His beloved children. These beings we raise might make things super hard—harder than we'd like—but man, let Jesus be Jesus. He will not leave or forsake your kids, no matter what.

Seek the wisdom of spiritual giants and the Word of Christ.

Chapter 11

A SHOULDER TO BLOW MY NOSE ON

Be happy with those who are happy,
and weep with those who weep.

ROMANS 12:15

No one seemed to understand what I was going through. Or so it seemed. But slowly, real people confessed. My favorite was Meredith, a neighbor while we were still living in town. She was in a different season—her only son was about to get married. Meredith is brilliant and wise and lives well.

One day, I was on a weeping walk. I went on them more often at that time. I would pray, barter, and sob.

Meredith and I were about to pass each other, and then we stopped. There was no escaping my sorrow.

I confessed, "We sent Luke to military school."

Meredith patted my shoulder, and then a smile spread across her ageless skin (seriously, it's like she doesn't have pores). She said, "Good for you!"

Wait, what?

Meredith let loose. "More parents should be so brave! Our son was a terror. We threatened but never went through with it. If I had a dollar for every time I saw that kid body-slammed and cuffed on the hood of a police cruiser, well, I would have been able to afford to send him to military school!"

Wait, what?

She told me more. Sneaking, stealing, and all things bad-boy. I couldn't reconcile these stories with what I knew of Meredith. She and her husband were church youth leaders. And wasn't her husband on the board of an at-risk youth organization?

If Meredith did have pores, they would radiate "chill." She is laid back, she paints, she frequents Ireland, and she survived an adolescent delinquent elegantly. To add to her spectacularness, she apologized to me. She apologized because she wished she had come to me when she first heard about Luke's troubles. She was sorry she hadn't been there for me. For us.

She lamented, "Moms should talk about it more. Instead, we take full responsibility and hide in shame."

You Can Run as Fast as Me

Not long ago, I was running errands in town with our foster-love Joy-Baby when my mommy helper, Miss Bobbi, texted to let me know Sam had been stung on his ear by a wasp. He was swollen and distraught but resting when I got home. I learned from Bobbi that moments before the vicious attack, Sam had been sweetly encouraging his younger brother, Charlie. He'd been cheering him on: "Ready, set, go! Come on, Charlie. You can run as fast as me!" Sam would fall slightly behind so his younger brother could catch him, and then they would race ahead together.

Without warning, Sam began to scream, and Bobbi rushed to his aid. Because the trio was out on the ranch hiking, they had a ways to walk back. Immediately, Charlie began to champion Sam, just as Sam had encouraged him. "We're almost home, Sam. You will be okay."

One encouraging another. One older, more experienced, bringing up the tail end. Then the younger encouraging the older, championing him and wishing him well.

I had the privilege of chatting with a talented blogger the other day, and we talked about mentor relationships. It occurred to me that although I am older than her, we have so much in common, and our conversation didn't convey that one of us knew more than the other. We are both on a journey.

We both benefited from our talk. We chirped back and forth about where we were in our writing, homeschooling, marriages, wellness, and the like. And while I shared some gems of advice with her, she did the same for me. Like Sam and Charlie's scenario, one started as the encourager, and then the other took that role. Isn't this a significant aspect of any relationship? The ebb and flow of inspiration, advice, laughter, tears, and cheer seem far more dynamic than the divisive relationship of mentor and protégé.

I have sought the counsel of a "spiritual mentor" before. It didn't go well. (For the most part, this was my fault.) Certainly, there are stewards of the Word of God from whom it would be good to seek direction, and Scripture encourages this. However, I propose that when we put a person in charge of our relationship with Jesus Christ, it ceases to be *our relationship*. And there is always the risk we will compare a mentor to our imagined ideal, or we will compare ourselves to that other woman.

Why is she so much closer to God than me? Does He prefer her over me? I am not having that experience...Does God love me as much as He loves her?

As mothers, I assume it makes sense to seek one another out for advice, but know this: Neither of you has all the answers. None of it is perfect.

I recall a mom from one of "those families." Rich, beautiful, thin—they were like a family out of a catalog. The couple was a little older than us, their two children (a boy and girl) a stage ahead of ours. Their Facebook pages were decorated with lofty achievements and fancy all-inclusive beach vacations (that are only applicable to families of four).

I didn't consider myself jaded when I recently saw that the couple's marriage ended because of his infidelity. However, I find it tragic how undone I was by the news, and how less shocked I was by the end of another, less affluent and less attractive couple's marriage. I compared and coveted, and I expected better things of those more affluent and more beautiful than me. As you might guess, I am fully willing to voice my ignorance.

The lowly place of missing Luke and the terror of wondering about his future made for one of the loneliest seasons of my life. Friends who were most genuine became most cherished. Gossips and "fake friends," eager to get the inside scoop, were easier to spot and even easier to ignore. Hypocrisy seemed more obvious. Betrayal stung more sharply. And in all of that, I was able to rest more and more in Jesus.

Straight to the Holy Spirit

The best spiritual advice I acquire is between me and the Holy Spirit. By accepting Christ as my own, I became entirely His. Certainly, there will be seasons of confusion or a need for wise counsel from others, but when Jesus died, the veil was torn. There's no longer any separation between His people and the holy of holies. God became—and remains—fully accessible to each of us, His children.

Sure, life coaches can have suggestions on organizing time or how to spice up a marriage, but when I hang up that phone, my life and relationships are still mine. In the last few years, I have sought the wisdom of some spiritual giants. I have been blessed, encouraged, and strengthened because of people who have walked a hard road before me. They have years' more experience than me and are well versed in Scripture. But they also encourage me to stay in the Word and to focus on believing God and seeking to know Him—not through the eyes of another believer, but directly through the eyes of He who adores me.

He will not let me down. He will not disappoint.

I recall the old church hymn "What a Friend We Have in Jesus." Truly, I thought this song was a joke. Prior to grace, steeped in the belief I had to earn Jesus's approval, He was not my friend. He was a taskmaster, impossible to please, ignorant of how hard I was "trying." He was confusing. One foot in the Old Testament and Jewish law and one foot in the New Testament and New Covenant.

I now understand these words by Joseph M. Scriven:

> What a friend we have in Jesus,
> all our sins and griefs to bear!
> What a privilege to carry
> everything to God in prayer!
> Oh, what peace we often forfeit,
> oh, what needless pain we bear,
> all because we do not carry
> everything to God in prayer!

Truly, this is a good friend. A dear and trusted friend. And no matter how dear and kind a human friend may seem, no one can compete with Jesus, who bears our grief and sin. A trusted confidant who is not motivated by gossip, greed, fear, or envy; someone who knew we couldn't, so He did. In the arms of this friend, stripped of false beliefs about Him, myself, my motherhood, and my life, I no longer forfeited peace, and my pain took on an entirely new meaning.

Go learn.

Go suffer.

Go stumble.

Go seek.

Go knock.

He will answer.

Chapter 12

SHOULDA, COULDA, WOULDA

Though [Christ] was God, he did not think of equality with
God as something to cling to. Instead, he gave up his
divine privileges; he took the humble position of a slave
and was born as a human being. When he appeared
in human form, he humbled himself in obedience
to God and died a criminal's death on a cross.

PHILIPPIANS 2:6-8

y phone buzzed. My friend had just sent me a video of a family with autistic twin sons. I don't pretend to know what it is like to have an autistic child. While John struggled in silence and Luke struggled in screeches, neither of them was trapped within the confines of their minds.

I hadn't slept well the night before and was having an emotional, frazzled day. But I watched the video a couple times. Even with my hazy mind, I knew there was something really important for me to grasp about this video.

In the video, the mom and dad explained that they had recognized "something was not right" when the boys were about two.

Neither of the kids would make eye contact or communicate. As time progressed, things continued to grow more dreadful. The boys were self-harming escape artists, and they destroyed everything in their reach. At a complete loss, the parents visited a couple of institutions. In the end, they determined they could not give up the boys.

The boys who brought disruption to the parents' lives were the very boys they couldn't fathom being away from. United, the parents asserted, "We can't give them up." Still, the boys terrorized the couple, destroying everything they owned, escaping from their home, and invoking manhunts and the use of search dogs. They were never relieved or even thankful for being returned home to the safety of their adoring mother and father.

Exasperated, yet committed, they learned about the Son-Rise Program, which is a surprising technique devised by the parents of a severely autistic child who made a full recovery in the 1970s. Their therapy program involves joining the children in their autistic behaviors rather than seeking to stop or modify them. The twins' father explained that one of the boys would not quit spinning, so he joined him. And right away, the son looked his father right in the eye—something the boy had never done before. Something the parents were told would never happen. As if by his father entertaining the behavior, the disabled boy recognized, *You understand me.* *

The breakthrough continued. By identifying with the boys, the mom and dad bridged the gap between "normal" and autistic.

Come Alongside

Jesus, who pursues us with faithfulness and fervor, came alongside us in our trials. He bridged the gap between human and holy. No, He didn't fall into sin as we do, but He was able to look at us

---

* https://youtu.be/-vXwNRCOzZM

and say, "I know." Jesus was with His people, so they weren't left alone in their struggles—and neither are we. In spite of every sacrifice, He loves unto His death.

Separation without a path of salvation was not an option. No matter what we soil, spit on, or give up on, He longs for our company. And when we stop and look into His eyes, we are connected forever.

Abraham was counted as faithful for his belief and obedience (see Genesis 15:6). This is parenting: to serve, toil, sweat, and bleed over a child who might not even acknowledge you when you walk into the room. Certainly, the twins in the video had an understanding of their parents' presence, but it was not until the parents modeled *their* understanding of the boys' erratic and wild behaviors—and still accepted them—that there was change. Only when the boys realized that their parents saw, knew, and understood them did they reciprocate love.

Under the law, continual failings separated humankind from a good and loving Father. Out of our minds and out of control, we were far from Him and miserable in our quest for completion. We banged our heads against the wall, broke windows, and climbed fences. We were hauled back time and again for our own safety.

The perfect love of God is patient and kind. He humbled Himself to experience a brutal and humiliating death. Why? Because separation without a path of salvation was not an option—even while we were still sinners, before we ever looked into His eyes and acknowledged His good and loving nature.

Still, There Is Love

God doesn't say to us "I love you because…" but rather, "Still, I love you. Still, nothing can separate you from Me."

Still, in spite of everything, I want to be with you.

Still, you are perfectly and wonderfully made.
Still, I will wait for you to turn to Me.

I love my kids. But would I love them if they couldn't show that they loved me back? Will I love them if they choose poorly or make a mistake with life-changing consequences?

Of course.

And if I love them like this, in all my imperfections, how much does my Father in heaven love me? How much does He love my kids?

Does God love Luke less because he struggled? Or Sophie more because she has natural abilities? Does He love a family with no debt, no health struggles, and the perfect marriage more than mine, which is the perfect opposite?

He Chooses Us All

The months that followed Luke's enrollment in military school were painful and enlightening. I wrote to him every day—really. His absence was deafening. I missed him desperately, and in his void, I recounted my failures and neglect.

Four months later, at Thanksgiving, we brought Luke home for a week. He was quiet, despondent. He seemed angrier than when we had dropped him off. I felt all the pangs of regret and failure. To add to our grief, we had just been notified that Charlie was being removed from our custody after 15 months. He was being placed with a relative.

Life was spinning out of control.

After dinner one night, I lay on the closet floor, staring at the ceiling. On the floor next to me were a psychology report on Luke, a notification from the state about Charlie's removal, and a rejection letter from a publisher who didn't think I was ready for publication because I wasn't "one thing." They wanted me to define a specific brand.

Broken.

That was the most logical brand I could identify with.

Justin didn't even come in the closet to check on me; he sim-ply went to bed. Certainly, we were an exemplary illustration of the American Christian family.

I prayed out of habit or desperation. And no help seemed to come. *How do You pick, God?* I prayed. *I am so broken, so weighed down. We are Christians. But everything here is a mess. Please tell me, how do You pick? Whom will You choose to help?*

And the answer came to my mind in a flash. It washed over me in utter perfection. I promise if I had only recorded the moment, I could play the words for you now. They were going to open the door to a whole new experience in Jesus Christ: "I choose all of you."

Just then, my phone lit up with a text from Justin: "I was just in the garage. Where is your car?"

Luke had been home less than 48 hours, and he had stolen my car.

As I drove Maggie's truck to the police station, my heart was heavy, but I wasn't hysterical. I was numb. *I choose all of you.* I held on to this.

At the police station, I explained that my car was missing, most likely taken by our son, who was home from military school and didn't have a license. They recommended an AMBER Alert. I filled out some papers, while an officer filled out another report.

"Mrs. Amerine, do you work?"

"I'm a stay-at-home mom and a foster mom. And I'm an author."

"So, you don't work?"

I looked at him. I didn't blink. I just stared a hole in his brain. He cleared his throat and said, "Uh, I mean, you do the hardest work. I just meant outside the home. I mean, you know, it's a thankless job but uh… You know, my wife always says…"

Stop talking, copper.

He coughed. "So, author, huh? What do you write about?"

A recent rejection letter flashed in my mind. What do I write about? Maybe *7 Easy Steps to Filling Out Your AMBER Alert Forms.*

"Um, I write…" I had no idea. I had no "brand."

He tried to help. "Like, do you write parenting advice?"

"No, *Detective*," I said, "it's two o'clock in the morning, and I'm standing in the police department in my pajamas because I can't find my son. I don't write parenting advice."

"Good point." He smirked. I filled out forms declaring my son "missing" and then sat in the truck and tried to cry.

I failed.

I drove home and slept like the dead until I heard the garage door in the early morning. I didn't bother to get up. I texted the officer, "He's home." Then I shut off my phone.

People are always really quick to give suggestions. "You should take his phone," for example. Lots of people have that idea.

No. If I take his phone, I am even less likely to be able to find him.

"You should…"

"I would…"

"We tried…"

I know these people mean well, but they don't know my son. I recall the desperate bargaining of the mother at the store: "Please, let's just check out, and I will buy you a sucker." Sometimes, as a mom, our only goal is to survive the moment.

Only Jesus

Everyone was stressed and sad. I was struggling to get a deep breath for myself, let alone breathe for everyone else. But this was new: From somewhere inside me, I knew I couldn't fix this for everyone. Everyone must grieve, everyone must stumble, and everyone must try to get up without my help. Yes, I can comfort and love and nurture. But if I fix everything for everyone, why do they need Jesus? If I'm meeting every single tear or whimper with warm chocolate chip cookies and physical and spiritual Band-Aids, when will they fall into the arms of their Jesus?

I lamented all the times I had tried to fix things for them. I can't do it. It's like lighting candles with the hope they will do more than just burn.

I have my grief. And I can't help but grieve as I watch those I love most also grieve. But I am not the balm to their souls like Jesus is. Today, in their darkest and scariest moments, I don't pray for God to give me the strength to fix them. I pray their hurt will be resolved by the One who died for them. Far from my arms...whether in their rooms alone, away at boot camp, or wandering and looking for answers...*Jesus, please be the name on which they call.*

Jesus, balm to my soul, take my kids further, deeper, and wider, to the places of healing not even this mom could know. I trust You to do what I cannot: heal the brokenhearted.

In that difficult time with Luke, I wrote myself a note to stick on my closet door: *Let Jesus be Jesus.*

A Soul Divided

Days later, we returned Luke to military school. That night, I climbed into bed, fully clothed. I accepted that my soul was spread seven ways at that moment. It was divided geographically and emotionally as my six children and one foster-love lived their lives. After an hour of tossing and turning, I tiptoed to my closet, got my computer, moved to my prayer chair, and wrote.

> Tonight, my soul is divided seven ways. One part is serving pizza and beer at a high-end joint downtown. One part is on a date that's not a date (but might be a date later, depending on how things go). One is 500 miles

away in a military bunk, with strangers who can dictate to him better than I. One part is at a stage production of *Footloose*, which is an event I would only enjoy if accompanied by Kevin Bacon. One part is pretending to read a book about planets and hopes to travel to the moon someday. One part is sound asleep in a crib in my office, and according to the state, he'll sleep in someone else's home in three days. And one part is drifting off to sleep in pink footed pajamas, wondering where her "real" mommy went.

It's easy to say, "It is well with my soul," when my whole soul is safely seated around my Sunday table for tender pot roast, potatoes, green beans, and apple pie. But on any given night, under any given moon, my soul is divided.

On any given night, under any given moon, my soul meets new people, tastes exotic foods, and may make choices that I would not. I cannot promise that it is always well with me. But my spirit is filled with good things. The Spirit that guides me in all things that are right, just, and pleasing, prays with me in words foreign to my understanding and symphony to my bones.

The next morning, while I sat and sipped my coffee, I heard Sophie pounding on the piano and singing Adele's "Hello" at the top of her lungs. Her voice was powerful, unlike my nasal and crackling one. She never stumbled on the keys as she pounded out the music *by ear*. John looked at me and smirked. "I don't know how she does that, but it would be awesome if we could get rich off it."

Indeed.

How does she do that? Where does that come from? Who in the world is she? Can I replicate this? Can I teach our adopted son this magic trick? No. It is hers. Her walk, her gift. I had nothing to do with it.

"I choose all of you…"

God does not hold me liable for Luke's struggles or Charlie's next step. He doesn't call me responsible for Sophie's talent; her abilities don't add to my salvation. Luke's struggles do not take away. And Charlie's impending removal wasn't a punishment or reward.

Instead, like the faithful parents in that video, God matches my motion. As I turn and spin, He does the same right next to me until my eyes meet His and I absolutely believe I am seen and known and loved as His daughter…still here on the sacred ground.

Let Him Be Luke

At Christmas, after seven months of military school, we made the decision to bring Luke home.

In a crazy turn of events, an acquaintance retained a lawyer on our behalf, and we won full custody of Charlie. We adopted him on October 31, 2015. We continue to have an open relationship with his birth family and his biological brothers.

Luke was happiest when he was with Maggie and John, who were both taking classes at Abilene Christian University. We continued to "homeschool" him with dual-credit classes at ACU. He was 16 going on 35. At six foot three, with a full red beard and a heart for babies and the homeless, he was a presence that had been wholeheartedly missed in our home. Yet he didn't want to stay.

Aside from an incident with an illegal tattoo from some rogue underground tattoo artist in a garage, he was basically compliant, but he couldn't stand the margins of high school or homeschool. In a brief altercation, we learned he had even met with a lawyer about being emancipated.

I know. Who does this?

Only Luke.

I wonder sometimes—how would Luke have functioned in a

different time or place? How would he have turned out if he'd been born in a grass hut in a village somewhere? I propose he would have taken off on long hikes looking for berries to be his meal and woodland animals to be his friends. I imagine the other grass-hut dwellers would be mad at him one minute for forgetting the firewood and celebrating him the next for fashioning a device to bring running water to the huts. Two hundred years ago, he would have been classified as middle aged, a landowner with seven kids of his own. But this was now, and this was here, and we had to do what we thought best for our son based on what we knew and what we hoped for him.

We let him go.

Luke's ACT scores were high enough to get him enrolled at ACU full time. We moved him into the dorms and let him be Luke. And let Jesus be Jesus.

On the evening Luke moved in, I wrote a new post on the blog: "Go, and Don't Believe Everything I Taught You…" I ended the post with this challenge to my children:

> I recognize *want* in these humans. They are curious; they crave more. And more is what I want for them. More than the story of David and Goliath as told by a cucumber and tomato.
>
> Go. Fight giants.
>
> More than a tale of a man, his boat, and wild beasts at sea.
>
> Go. Live your life without a care for the naysayers and hecklers, and take in a few strays along the way.
>
> More than legends of seas being parted and walls tumbling down.
>
> Go. Speak boldly and by all means…lead.
>
> More than an anecdote of a man spending an entire night in a lions' den and living to tell the tale.

Go. Be brave.

More than a bedtime story of a girl who became queen and saved her people.

Go. Stand up for right and wrong. Fight for the weak ones. Fear your conscience more than consequences.

More than a yarn of a prophet swallowed by a whale.

Go to the dark places. Go to the depth of solitude. Go and spend time pondering what went wrong.

And oh, how I pray that the account of the virgin birth, death, and resurrection of a Jewish carpenter is written on your soul. And I beg you hear His name whispered on the wind and waves, "Jesus."

Go and *believe.*

Go learn. Go suffer. Go stumble. Go seek. Go knock. He will answer. When you're in need, He will be in wait. And when you are ready, He will be more than a story— He will be yours.

Oh, how much I love my God. I hope I did well in modeling that for you. But alas, that was me. And this is you. So go, deny that which you find hard to believe. Go and dig for answers. Go and ask the hard questions. Go climb mountains, swim seas, and trek through deserts in search of that which will fill you up so that you never grow thirsty.

I'll wait here.

I will continue to pray for you. I will pray for safety. I will pray for wisdom. I will pray. And when you have all your answers, please come home and tell me all about the adventures that led you to your God.

It is a story I cannot wait to hear.[1]

This parenting gig is catch and release. Yes, they are my sons; no, I don't want them to need me. I can't go with them.

Chapter 13

CATCH AND RELEASE

*The faithful love of the LORD never ends! His
mercies never cease. Great is his faithfulness;
his mercies begin afresh each morning.*

LAMENTATIONS 3:22-23

The morning I put John on a plane to go to the School of
Infantry, we knew that the next time we would see him, in four
months, he'd have completed his schooling and would be ready
for…battle. The two of us had dinner alone the last night he was
home, and we talked about things. Hard things, some things I didn't
want to hear.

*Dear John, how did you become a marine? How did I ever become
this mom who is not utterly horrified at the idea of your being a marine?
As a testimony to how much I have finally let go and believed God, I
want you to go.*

At dinner that last night, he said, "I hope I get to throw real
grenades."

And I said, "Me too." For the record, I also said, "I hope you
throw them hard and far. Very, very, very far."

The next day, I waited for him to call all afternoon. I knew he would get to make one phone call to let us know he arrived. He would have his phone taken from him, but first, he would be instructed to notify family he was safe and sound.

The call never came.

As a testimony to how hard I am working at letting go, I texted his redheaded sweetheart.

She got the call.

My reaction is probably not what you think—not at all.

Get Out of Their Way

During my mother-in-law's last weeks of illness and life, she grew in wisdom and grace. Granted, we had our history. Iris did, in fact, threaten to have me killed days before my wedding. We had baggage, but in her journey from this earth to her heavenly home, we found unity, and I cherish the memory of those last weeks. During the day, I would school the children, and she would hold Sam. We were pleasant, and she was grateful for the care. She thanked me and complimented me, and I loved serving her.

At night, I slept beside her. About 20 minutes after taking her medicine, she would sleep-criticize me about stuff she had warehoused during the day: "Jami! The gravy is lumpy!" or "Jami! You're getting fatter!" or "Jami! If you don't give Sam a bath, I'll turn you in to Child Protective Services!" I giggled. I had her cell phone, so she wouldn't be turning me in *again*.

But she also said things that offered clarity. Once, after a beloved Baptist minister from her past stopped by for a visit, she said, "I have something to tell you, but don't tell Justin." I agreed, and she continued, "Jami, I'm Baptist. I converted to Catholicism, but I don't believe you have to do all the things to get to heaven. I think Jesus loves me exactly as I am." Another time she said, "If Jesus needed me to do all the things, why would He have died? Why not just tell me to do all the things?"

Granted, she wasn't a Bible scholar, but she was indeed closer to truth than I was. I kept these moments and counted them among my favorite memories in my journey as Justin's wife, Iris's daughter-in-law. A week later, as I struggled to shower her, she said, "Jami, put this in your book. Tell everyone I said, 'Let your sons marry decent wives, and *get out of their way.*'"

At the time I had never written a word. I had no plans to write anything.

But now that I have you here... Let your sons marry decent wives and get out of their way.

Iris herself missed that memo until the last few days of her life. She wanted Justin to stay her baby. She didn't like me. I refused to bathe the children with a quarter cup of bleach in their bathwater. My chili had kidney beans in it, which mystified and infuriated her. She called it "Yankee chili." But I loved her boy, and I still do. And unbeknownst to her, he loves kidney beans in his chili.

I understand that Iris didn't want to share her boy. Sharing children is one of the more challenging passages of motherhood; I can sympathize now. John and Luke love me so much; Sam and Charlie are my biggest fans. But something changes when they fall in love. One minute, sons are wholly yours; the next, they are wholly...not. Christy Mobley once described it to me as a kidnapping, or being fired from the best job ever. In a blog post of hers she expressed the process of letting go in this way:

> We prepared them for this, didn't we? We prepared our
> children to walk, talk, make friends and share toys. We
> put them on their first bike and pushed them off on their
> way. We explained how to be a good sport when they won
> and when they lost. We prepared them to drive and gave

them the means by which to do it. We got them ready for
prom and taught them about love and heartbreak. But in
all this preparation, did we prepare for our own heart to
break when it came time to let them go?... As mommas,
we're geared to rear. It's in our nature to nurture. But if life
is to continue and God's beauty [be] reproduced, some
things must come to an end if others are to flourish.[1]

I remember what it felt like for Justin to pull away from his mom,
only to have her dig in even more. Why go to all the trouble of raising such a good and decent man if you only want to lock him in his
childhood bedroom? As my boys turned into man-babies, I had to
remember that this parenting gig is catch and release. Yes, they are
my sons; no, I don't want them to need me. I can't go with them.
(Well, pieces of me will go with them. And I hope it's the respectable
parts—not the fragments where I drove like a mad woman to bas-
ketball practice. Hopefully not the pieces where I cried on the floor
of the laundry room because the laundry literally is never caught up,
ever, and I threatened never to buy Cheetos again if they all continued to wear and dirty their clothes.)

On the way to John's graduation from marine boot camp, his
sweetie and I watched a couple online videos about boot camp graduation protocol. The man in the video said, "Marine moms have
priority over marine girlfriends. You gals keep your eyes shut until
momma sees her marine. You can hug him second. You don't count
today, girls." We would hear a similar message at Marine 101.

Moms first. I know it's a tradition, and it's all in good fun, but
what do I want for my son? Do I really want him to seek me out
before this beautiful redhead he's like-liked since the fifth grade?
Would I rather have his immediate attention, or would I rather him
finish strong? Would I prefer he look forward to my company or
dread his duty to give me the first hug? What is the point of all this
parenting if he still needs me close?

What is the entirety of motherhood?

What are we raising up these children for?

Jesus's Mama

God has ministered to me in the sweetest way through the message of Mary, Jesus's mother. As I read her story in Scripture, I find myself wanting to know so much more about her. I wish I could grab her and give her a big squeeze, hand her a cup of tea, and start asking questions.

Was Jesus easy to potty train?

Would He eat his broccoli?

Did you know? Like, did you really understand what was going to happen?

How'd you do it? How did you keep yourself at the cross?

Mary didn't have superpowers. If she had, wouldn't she have changed the water into wine herself? Wouldn't she have spared her son the ministry that led to His death? Instead of imagining her robed in blue, hands folded in prayer before the infant Jesus, I like to think of her as a young mom—short, chubby, Palestinian—barking at Jesus to eat His soup. Ponder the fatigue of an outcast, running for her life and the life of her child, ever indebted to the man who listened to God and took her as his wife at all costs. I like to think of her twelve years later, having misplaced the Son of God, worried sick and crying and barely understanding how her child could be in a different Father's house.

I can identify, to an extent, with Mary the mom. So I have made it a habit to ask myself, "What would Mary do?" To contemplate Christ through the eyes of His mother, as a mother yourself, is truly enlightening. Imagine watching one of your children suffering the injustice, the torture, of a crucifixion, and feel yourself being pitched into her nightmare.

But she knew it was never about her; it was about Him. Her heart would be pierced along with His side, but she knew her heart would be pierced for the good of the world.

Owed Nothing, Given Much

My son didn't call me first. He called his girlfriend.

What would Mary do?

She would remember that John's work and accomplishments were not about her.

I am of the mind-set that my children owe me nothing. We've all heard horrible mother-in-law stories, and the common denominator is about something owed to them. A debt of services. I don't feel I deserve something from my kids, nor do I want them to feel obligated to repay me.

The need my kids have for me will lessen. I see that happening already. Perhaps that is the struggle for most of us mothers as we let go or refuse to do so, afraid we will cease to be important, cease to be needed. Meanwhile, my need for Christ increases.

Who are we? Vessels that bring life. But who gives that life through us? Christ, to whom we owe everything, and who asks nothing of us in return for our salvation except for faith in Him.

In our family we have a saying: "Expect nothing from anyone but Jesus. He won't let you down." The freedom of expecting no praise, no gifts, and no worship for myself affords me the blessing of genuine praise, gifts, and worship given to God. I am reminded of the last part of the prayer of St. Francis, "It is in giving that we receive; it is in pardoning that we are pardoned; and it is in dying that we are born to everlasting life."

If you are in hysterics because you didn't get a card for Mother's Day, what do you need that you cannot get from Jesus? Accolades? Because He adores you. Praise? God thinks you're the bomb.

Thanks? He is glad for your tender, loving care of the least of these. God isn't like the demanding mother-in-law from a bad joke. No— He's wild about you.

Hers, Mine, and Ours

On the day I waved goodbye to John and waited in vain for his call, I asked myself what Mary would do. I reminded myself of the truth I knew.

Late that night, I was working and trying to keep my thoughts from slipping into the mom-sulk mire. I happened to look down at my phone. It remained silent, but this time, the screen was lit up with the words, "Missed call from John. Voice mail from John."

I picked up the phone and quickly accessed my messages.

"Hey, Mom. I've been trying to reach you and Dad since I landed. Your phone's going straight to voice mail. I finally called Anne and asked her to let you know I am here safe. Thank you for everything. I'll be in touch. I have my phone until roll call in 25 minutes if you get this… I hope I can talk to you. I love you."

I called him right back. He'd sent text messages and called. After I hung up with my son and rebooted my phone, all his messages came through, including the message from Anne. It would be a nice collection to read and listen to during the painfully slow few weeks he would be away from any communication device.

Do I love him more knowing he did in fact call?

No.

Am I glad he acknowledges me? Of course.

My phone was blowing up with messages. So were my social media accounts. Maggie and her fiancé, Christian, had just eloped and announced it on Facebook. Everyone wanted to know if she was pregnant or if I was upset.

No, she wasn't pregnant.

No, I wasn't upset. In fact, I encouraged my daughter to elope—and I wish I'd been so bold as to do the same myself a few decades ago.

An elopement isn't the norm, of course. Right now in Texas, the trend is shabby chic, outdoor furniture, cake and barbecue, and a sparkler send-off event. So that was sort of what we were thinking when Maggie got engaged. Sort of. I should have been more excited—I am, in fact, a certified florist and wedding planner—but I just wasn't feeling it.

One day, shortly after Maggie and Christian were engaged, they came home from her childhood friend's wedding, and Maggie said, "It was beautiful; it was perfect—but it's not what I want."

Cha-ching.

Seriously though, it wasn't about the money. It was about Maggie. Her trademark "look" as a child was frilly skirts and shirts, impossibly enormous hair bows, and a bag of bugs and worms. This has never been a kid who cared about what everyone else was doing. She deserved her own kind of wedding.

We were headed to San Diego for marine boot camp graduation, and she and Christian were staying an extra week for a college friend's wedding. So I suggested they get married on the beach.

Maggie and Christian, who met while studying abroad in England, actually ended up having a darling ceremony on the balcony of the Santa Barbara courthouse. Then they had a progressive "reception" with gluten-free cake at a little bakery downtown. And they are happy. This is what suited them. This was their dream wedding. A $17 white sundress she purchased off Amazon and money in their pockets to travel.

These kids. They are wanderlust and adventure.

I received six emails extending condolences. "I know you are disappointed not to get to do a huge wedding for your baby, but remember, it's not about the wedding—it's about the marriage." I appreciated my friends' concern—truly—but I was over the moon. That unconventional courthouse wedding was exactly what Maggie and Christian wanted.

I have always loved when my kids were able to do something unique. Not for me, but for them. When Maggie was in the eighth grade, my parents moved to Kazakhstan. To be honest, I knew nothing of this place, but I knew Maggie should go with them. We made arrangements for her to go with them for eight weeks. I love Maggie, we missed her, but the opportunities to read Russian literature and watch DVDs of *Jeopardy!* with my mom? Who would want to miss that?

Maggie ate crème brûlée at a café near the Eiffel Tower; she had Belgian waffles in Belgium; she tasted horse meat and caviar. She had someone try to purchase her from my parents in Amsterdam. The event sparked within her an interest in combating human sex trafficking. For her senior homeschool thesis, she wrote a paper on the topic, and then, as a capstone, she organized a 5K to raise money for the Red Thread Movement, which provides fair-trade work for women all over the world. She raised nearly $3,000.

And John? Before leaving for boot camp, he was living in the guesthouse here on the ranch. One time while he was there, he texted me and asked if we had any food. I told him I was in Abilene at the grocery store, but I wouldn't be home for a couple hours.

When I arrived home, I offered him the bounty of my grocery bags, and he said, "I already ate."

"What did you eat?" I asked.

"I shot a rabbit off the back porch with my bow and arrow," he said. "I sautéed it in butter, and then I made gravy with the drippings. I found a can of fridge biscuits to go with it. There's a little left if you want some."

Rabbit, biscuits, and gravy, y'all.

Hard pass.

This man is six foot four, and he looks like a Norse god. He's barely able to read, but if you're in a tight spot, this is the man you call. In any situation, he's your best bet.

And Luke? I recently asked him, "Do you resent the time you spent at military school?" He scoffed, "No way! None of my friends know how to count off military marching. That's legit street creds." I would also interject the old saying, "If you love someone let them go…" Luke lives with us again. He cooks beautiful vegan meals. He plays cards with the Vandals and watches horror flicks with Sophie. As I type this he is in the front yard with Justin, trimming a tree. In our current home search, he requested to have his own bathroom. Justin and I looked at each other; I mean he's nearly nineteen. I said, "Certainly, are your planning on staying with us for a while?" He flashed enormous dimples and said, "Oh yeah! I love it here!"

What makes one kid a success? What earns one set of parents kudos and accolades? What achievements make us point to a grown child and tell the parents, "You did something right"? Every child is an individual. There isn't a formula for this—there's only the kid in front of you.

Perhaps the goal and achievement are simply loving well. And the ultimate Christian education—the child's search for Christ— has to be his or her own. Sometimes, oftentimes, the only answer is freedom.

The message of grace is spreading like wildfire.

Chapter 14

PHILOSOPHIES, LEGALITIES, AND SINGING RACCOONS

God sent his Son into the world not to judge the
world, but to save the world through him.

JOHN 3:17

When Maggie was in kindergarten, I and several other über-conservative moms were part of the "Boycott Disney" crowd. I held tight to my belief that the untimely death of nearly every mother figure in Disney history was part of a political war raging against the family.

I don't know...I had a lot more time on my hands.

It was the Tuesday before Thanksgiving when the school called. Maggie's teacher informed me that Maggie was in hysterics. Apparently, the kindergarten and first-grade classes were taking advantage of the half day and were going to have popcorn and watch Disney's *Pocahontas*. Mrs. Campbell explained, "Maggie is very upset, and I am wondering if you can please explain why she cannot watch *Pocahontas*."

"Yes, she cannot watch that movie. We feel Disney has taken a true historical event and morphed it into a romanticized version of sheer nonsense. Why? What did Maggie say?"

Mrs. Campbell noted, "She said she is not allowed to watch it because raccoons don't sing."

(Also, it was recently brought to my attention that there are no singing raccoons in *Pocahontas*.)

There are things you hold dear, convictions you cling to, things you want to instill in your children. Know this: They will probably only retain about 11 percent of it. The rest, well…the rest they will develop on their own. Maggie knew she wasn't supposed to watch Disney movies, but she had no real understanding of why.

I'd spent the day teaching preschool and changing diapers when one of my college kids came home in need of advice. She asked for help with a paper. It was on adoption for homosexual couples, and specifically on a friend of hers that wanted to adopt. I won't go into details, but an argument ensued.

Another tween in the house chimed in, "Who are we to say it is a sin?"

We are a conservative family. We pray and go to church together. Justin and I were floored by that comment. Tears were shed. My husband went outside to cool his head. Then we reconvened, taking turns, discussing biblical truths and how it used to be.

But during this argument, my kids weren't thinking about biblical truths. They were not considering standards or beliefs or concepts. They were thinking about their friends—people with names and faces and spirits. They were thinking about a struggling young man who loves Jesus. The issue isn't his sexuality; it's his heart.

Our child lamented, "These are my friends. I go to school with them. I go to church with them. They may be wrong, but they are told they are right. I love these human beings, and I don't think they are wrong. Love is love."

And I can empathize. I have family and friends in committed homosexual relationships, and they are welcome at my table. But I still believe God created them for more.

When Justin and I started our parenting journey, the closet door was still tightly shut. You didn't see gay couples on soap operas, and they certainly were not championed. Raising children seemed simple back then: "Don't say 'shut up.' Boys marry girls. Don't litter. Don't cuss." Today, it's more complicated. God designed sex between a man and a woman—that is biologically evident. But we are no longer witnesses from afar.

My husband and I have had a new realization. Our babies are on the front lines.

Christ in Us

Justin and I did not prepare to sit in church and hear a sermon on how sin was changing. We did not prepare to have our child invited to a slumber party where the birthday boy had two mommies. Nor did we prepare for homosexual men and women to become part of our family circle.

At a recent Christian writers conference, I met with six different published authors. Beautiful, wise believers, all of them. When I told them about this chapter, *four* of them confessed they had an adult son or daughter involved in a homosexual lifestyle. Of the children who have come out of the closet, how many of their parents have nowhere to turn? None of us prepared for this.

I know I'm not going to change any minds with this chapter. This topic has been discussed plenty. I know what I believe, and you know the same. So why bother discussing it in a book about the parenting journey?

Because the kids are on the front lines. They're the ones who will carry truth to generations not yet born. We need to teach them truth, and we need to teach them *love*. And love, too often, is what the church is missing.

I stand by this: If we are so judgmental as to exclude groups of human beings from the church, how are we the hands and feet of Jesus? Furthermore, was there a single incident in Scripture where Jesus Christ refused to be in the midst of a particular group? No, He broke bread with tax collectors and prostitutes. It was among shunned sinners He was most effective in showing His character— love. If Christ is in us and working through us, if our identity is truly in Him, then His love becomes our way of being. That's our hope. That's our living faith.

From my seat on Sunday morning, my heart breaks for the pastor faced with the near-impossible choice of speaking truth or dividing a congregation. *Do I call sin by name? Or do I preach a softball sermon?* I see the agony of the youth minister as he is faced with a young person questioning her sexuality. He signed on to teach the kids about Jesus, and if he chooses to speak the truth about God's design, the teenager could very well decide that church isn't for her— and never come back.

The battlefield is different from what it used to be. The war cry is not the same. I write this not to provoke an argument, but as a reminder that in the midst of our arguing, there are real people at stake. We can no longer be so polarized as to negate human feelings or the commandment we were left with: "Love one another" (1 John 3:23).

Loving as Moms Do

A few days after the argument, I went to coffee with some old friends. At this table sat six Christian women. I knew one of them had a son in drug rehab. We were struggling with a financial crisis and Luke. One of them had just buried her daughter-in-law and was helping her widowed son with three littles under the age of four.

One of them has a child involved in a homosexual relationship; she champions his rights. Another also has a child in a homosexual relationship; she is crushed. Another's daughter had just miscarried for the fifth time.

There are polite ways to speak around the struggles—to be politically correct, if you will. But we are united in this: We are all moms. We all want our babies to be okay. We've spent every ounce of energy we have to make it so.

One of the women brought up homosexual marriage. There was an awkwardness, an uneasiness. A gap in what is okay. What is the truth? Both moms of gay sons can quote Scripture at each other—words intended to bless, not curse, but which make them cry anyway.

"My son is a good person. Why shouldn't he be allowed to marry and have a family?"

"My son is such a disappointment. He's wealthy and successful, but he's steeped in sin."

I believe that God created marriage between man and woman. Still, the commandment He left me was to love. My eyes burn with tears for the struggles of all these women, not for my opinion.

What is the answer?

Yeah, I know you just yelled your answer at this book, but I would bet you a box of Cheez-Its your answer was influenced by someone you love. Mine is. Please, bear with me. For a moment, let the thing that cannot divide us be our motherhood. Can you not sympathize? And if you cannot, can you pray that you might?

Speaking the Truth Without Love

As I composed this, I prayed fervently on how to approach this topic. We've become so polarized that we can't listen to each other without turning our discussion into a fight. A popular blogger, for example, has a platform directed at the sin of homosexual behaviors. With over 400,000 followers on Facebook alone, her posts invoke praise and outrage at viral rates. But who is she talking to in the name of Jesus? Other people who already agree with her. She is preaching to a self-righteous choir. And while I'm sure that her hard work gets petitions signed, I doubt it heals or helps those who are really hurting or lost.

Love one another.

We were created for love. We were created to love one another. From a place of believing that God is love and we are more than our struggles, we can be most effective in ministering and nurturing. None of us—not you, not me, not our husbands, not our children—is defined by our sexual experiences. All of us are defined by our response to Christ.

A young man we know was raised in a conservative home by Christian parents. They had disowned him years before when he'd entered into a relationship with another man. But with his grandparents' seventy-fifth anniversary and a huge family gathering approaching, the parents wanted to be reconciled with their son— at least long enough for the family photo. They wanted to present their son and diffuse any questions. Their handy way of dealing with this: They required their son to sign a document denying Christ.

I'll let you read that again.

Their ultimatum was, *You can be around us and be gay, as long as you stop being a Christian.*

I am certain if one of my children were struggling with this, the last thing I would want would be him or her giving up on Jesus.

A Generation Apart

I remember telling my children about God. We watched Veggie-Tales. We memorized scriptures and sang catchy songs. We boycotted

Disney, homeschooled, unschooled, and ate organic spinach. In the midst of all the good I did right, they witnessed everything I did wrong. They must have been so confused. From one side of my mouth, I taught them words from the Bible. From the other side, I was panicked, worried, and judgmental.

"If my mom loves Jesus, and Jesus conquered the world, why is she hysterical all the time?"

Allow me to step on to my soapbox for a second. I often hear the millennials referred to as "a generation wasted." Our generation needs to leave them alone and stop making fun of their worthless screen time while posting on *our* screens about how wayward they are.

I propose the younger generation is going to profess the truth of Jesus Christ like no generation before them.

Based on millennials I know, I believe them to be a brilliant generation. They can spot an ad campaign from two feet away. They aren't falling for our puffed-up religiosities or our mixed-up versions of Jesus. They are privy to our Americanized hypocrisy, and they are kinder, more compassionate, and more transparent than any generation before them.

All is not lost.

God knows them. He knows their names.

And from the convictions I have witnessed among this age group, God will be declared in the rawest form for who He is. The message of grace is spreading like wildfire. Coincidence? Hardly. In its simplest form, grace is best described in one word, *the* Word: Jesus. Jesus, who is love.

Salt and Light

On the Sunday after our family argument, we invited Maggie, John, Luke, and their college gang to lunch at our home. As the kids sat around the table, laughing, grabbing seconds of mashed pota-toes, yeast rolls, and cake and cookies, I sat in wonder.

I know these kids. I love these kids. A thief on one side, a sin-gle mother-to-be on the other, and a young man involved in a sex-ual relationship with another young man—all of them buttering my most excellent yeast rolls. They are all welcome here. What they didn't know that day was that they broke bread with me: a stress binge-eater who charges things at Kohl's behind her husband's back and has a susceptibility toward doughnuts when she is sad. We are all sinners.

But I want to believe that it wasn't and isn't so easy to sway the children from how we raised them. At that moment, I had seven kids. Surely one of them embraced what we have taught them? After the visitors returned to the dorms with bellies full of homemade goodness, we discussed the argument we'd had the previous week. And one of our teens said, "Personally, I think it is wrong. I stand by the biblical teaching that man should not lie with man. And I think I will be bringing up children in a drastically different world than I was brought up in. I worry about the future of the church."

Ha! Someone was listening. And then he said, "This is the most un-disappointing chair experience I have had in my life. It's like I am sitting on a cloud. I think we should incorporate more of this chair and some spray cheese into my schedule."

I am in charge of salt and light, folks.

Christic is

our purity.

Chapter 15

SIMPLY LOVING WELL

*Who then will condemn us? No one—for
Christ Jesus died for us and was raised to life
for us, and he is sitting in the place of honor
at God's right hand, pleading for us.*

ROMANS 8:34

At John's boot camp graduation, one of his very closest friends made a bad decision on Family Day, shoplifting a marine fridge magnet. He was given an NJP (a non-judicial punishment) that barred him from graduation. He had gone the entire way, completed the Crucible (a three-day endurance test), did everything right—and then, in a moment, lost it all. He is not a marine; his dream is gone. He was isolated from his company. John witnessed some of the company yelling at him, making fun of him. This young man had lost every earthly thing he'd worked for in an instant. By marine standards, he was nothing.

I knew John must have been upset about this. I asked him, "Are you okay?"

John scoffed and said, "You are either a marine, or you're not.

You either have integrity, or you don't." In the Marine Corps, there is no room for division. You need to be able to trust your brothers.

I cannot explain how I have grieved for this recruit, stripped of all his efforts, friendships, and goals because of his folly. And I know he messed up. Believe me, I am not asking the Marine Corps to start lowering the bar on integrity. But when I spied John's friend leaning up against a building as his company carried out their war bags and headed home as marines, he looked so young, so broken, so sad. For a moment, I pictured him as a boy pretending to be a marine. I saw him running, playing, dreaming of saving the world—innocent, unaware of what can be lost in a moment of the flesh. I started to cry.

Crying at graduation is the norm, yet I wept not for the pride, but for the anguish. I wanted to go and get him and say, "This does not define you. This is not the sum of who you are. This is not the last."

John looked at me out of the corner of his eye forebodingly, and we got in the car and drove away.

You either are a marine or you're not.

The Sin That Defines You

John saw his friend's error in completely black-and-white terms (or said he did.) *You are or you aren't.* Tragically, this is the same attitude many Christians have about sexual purity. In the views of many in the church, God can forgive any sin except sexual sin. Sex outside of marriage dirties you forever. This is the sin that defines you.

Friend, you've been washed in the blood, dunked in the water, and *that's* what defines you.

This message is for every woman who reads this, but I pray it carries over into a better version of how we raise up our children in their sexuality. You are not defined by your virginity. You are not defined by the loss of your virginity, whether by choice or by force.

Your purity ring doesn't define you. Your creepy step-uncle, curious neighbor, or best friend's perverted brother—they do not define you. The only thing that defines you is a *yes* to Jesus Christ. You are redeemed. You can't be unredeemed. No, never.

You are no longer defined by sex; you are defined by your belief. For a minute, can you not see what Christ sees? And if you cannot, can you see what Mary saw? Her baby slaughtered for the masses, for this battle, for this very struggle, for your baby. When we portray Jesus Christ from a place of utter disgust and self-righteousness, we are misrepresenting Him. Indeed, He said, "Go and sin no more" (John 8:11). But He was speaking directly to one woman about one specific sin. To us, He said we should be taking the logs out of our own eyes before we attempt to take the specks out of our neighbors' (see Matthew 7:5).

Purity. We talk about celibacy and chastity like they're the keys to the kingdom. Pure mouths, pure hearts, and pure malarkey. Some churches have imposed on their children new "laws" about courtship that are not found in Scripture, going so far as to say a couple shouldn't kiss until they're pronounced husband and wife.

In our desperate attempt to validate and define our children as "pure," we have bred a generation of sneaks and liars. Here in the Bible Belt, especially in more conservative circles, I have witnessed this in epic proportions. I watched a similar situation on Facebook among some acquaintances. Family A's son is marrying Family B's daughter, and the families bragged about how the couple was waiting for their wedding day for their first kiss. They filmed the darling, albeit staged, marriage proposal. The adorable couple "side hugged" and awkwardly high-fived each other, and all four proud parents could be heard giggling and saying, "Bet that first kiss would feel good right about now."

Funny.

I and several other people have witnessed this same couple

engaged in full-blown heavy petting behind the coffee shop. Also, three movie theaters, Dollar General, Taco Bell, and none of us can even face what happened on the hood of their car at McDonald's. But for the sake of their parents and the laws of the purity culture, the young people put on a false front. A great way to start any marriage, the foundation a lie.

Elizabeth Smart was 14 years old when she was abducted from her Salt Lake City home in the middle of the night. She was held captive and, for the nine months until she was rescued, faced daily violent sexual assaults by her captor.

In a 2016 interview, Smart vocalized her concerns for girls raised in a purity culture.

> I did make that promise to myself that I was going to wait until marriage before I had sex… Well, then I was kidnapped and I was raped, and one of the first thoughts I had was, *No one is ever going to want to marry me now: I'm worthless, I'm filthy, I'm dirty.* I think every rape survivor feels those same feelings, but having that with the pressure of faith compounded on top—it was almost crippling.[1]

So many of us have faced assault, abuse, or an event outside our control. Many more of us have just succumbed to core passions that changed us physically and mentally. But Christ is our purity. The kudos you may receive as parents of someone who has "never been kissed" cannot hold a candle to the righteousness bought for your baby on Calvary.

Humans are sexual. This was part of God's perfect design made imperfect by man. We are not defined or made whole by our sexual experience or inexperience.

The continual issue of sex through the ages—what's hot, what's not; what's wrong, and what's right—will leave us all barking at the moon. We cannot fish for men with nets full of hate and condemnation. The desire to change, the desire to seek truth, comes from a place where we are loved and understood.

A mother should never feel beaten down or shamed by her children's choices. Of course, sex should be delayed until marriage, and you certainly don't want your baby burdened with the pain of an immature or violent sexual encounter. Yes, teach your children that sex is for marriage, but please, do not feel shame should they choose otherwise—and by all means, don't let their sexuality be a feather in your cap. Truly, think about this: Do you really believe parents should be praised because their kid is a virgin? This is no more an ode to a parent's greatness than Sophie's ability to play the piano by ear is to mine.

This is my heart's cry: To parent well, we must *be* parented perfectly. We can accomplish this by letting Jesus be Jesus. Our relationships are made up of human beings who are loved by a God who knows their name.

To every mother of a child struggling with drugs, violence, disability, sex, academics, morality—issues that are judicial, spiritual, or imaginary—I join you in prayers for wisdom. (Wisdom is most often all we know to ask for.) All is not lost.

You may feel that your child has been isolated and stripped of his achievements—just like the young recruit leaning against the wall. But Jesus is not surprised, taken aback, horrified, or shocked. He walks up to your child and acknowledges him or her by name. Jesus came to bind up the brokenhearted, to heal, and to guide in ways we had not known. Imagine Him taking your baby's hand and showing that child life abundant.

Let Jesus be Jesus.

Let Jesus be everything your child needs. Speak your piece, step back, and let them stumble and fall, fully believing the world was conquered by the cross. Take a deep breath right now and fill your lungs with glorious truth. Christ is seated at the right hand of the Father, and in the light of His grace, *all* sin falls away.

My sister, Stacey Todd, often replaces *love* with *Jesus* in 1 Corinthians 13:4-7. It reads like this:

> *Jesus* is patient and kind. *Jesus* is not jealous or boastful or proud or rude. *Jesus* does not demand *His* own way. *Jesus* is not irritable, and *He* keeps no record of being wronged. *Jesus* does not rejoice about injustice but rejoices whenever the truth wins out. *Jesus* never gives up, never loses faith, is always hopeful, and endures through every circumstance.

This love—this Jesus love—moves us toward compassion. From that place of compassion, God will lead us to love well, free from condemnation and worry, guiding in ways of wholeness and restoration on the sacred ground.

Your belief in Jesus is the thermostat for your home.

Chapter 16

SHE SEEMS FAMILIAR

Anyone who belongs to Christ has become a new
person. The old life is gone; a new life has begun!

2 CORINTHIANS 5:17

M r. Darcy was a rescue kitten. He was a long-haired Sia-
mese with blue eyes, and he was every bit as snobbish and
exclusive as his literary namesake. Maggie, who was about
12 years old when we brought him home, was isolated by our location on our family ranch and by the fact that we homeschooled. Mr.
Darcy was her best friend.

He would lie on her bed while she did her schoolwork, and he
would follow her on her walks on the ranch. The girl–cat duo was
inseparable—or so she thought. Apparently, Mr. Darcy had a life
Maggie was oblivious to.

One afternoon, Maggie came bolting into the kitchen from the
backyard. She was hysterical, and I could barely make out what she
was saying. Through her sobs, I was able to surmise something was
wrong with Mr. Darcy. I followed the howling Maggie out to the
pool house, where Mr. Darcy was curled up on a beach towel, nurs-
ing seven newborn kittens.

Mr. Darcy was a Mrs.

And now he—er, she—was also a mother.

In spite of the passel of kittens Maggie would come to adore, the child fully believed she had been lied to. Slowly, she let go of the self-made lies and embraced the living, breathing gift of the truth. She had her beloved female cat, Mr. Darcy, and a crowd of new furry friends. It was a good trade.

"What's in a Name?"

Names are important to me. My entire life, when asked how to spell Jami, the inquirer spells out, "J-a-m-i-e?" and I rotely respond, "No *e*." And then they ask, "No *e*?"

That's right, no *e*.

They ask as if I have made a mistake. "Are you sure you know how to spell your name?" Yup, pretty sure. I am a terrible speller, but I know my own name.

My mom actually offered to have an *e* added when I was 12. But the truth was, I was Jami with no *e*. I didn't want to be known as anyone different.

Would an *e* at the end of my name have changed who I was at the core? No. Would Maggie still have all the qualities we adore if she were Piper? Yes. Was Mr. Darcy still able to birth kittens in spite of her male name? Apparently.

Sure, names can define us. From the first time someone called me "Mom" or called me by my new last name after my marriage—that halting moment someone said, "Mrs. Amerine?"—I was different. The miracles that happened in those moments cannot be undone. Names matter. To be known—isn't that what we all long for?

But if I ceased to be called "Mom," if I were no longer a wife, if I added the name "Grandma" to my repertoire, would any of that change my identity as a daughter of Christ? No. Because that's the part of my identity that matters for eternity. It is who we are when we are named daughters and sons of Christ that matters most.

Beloved Girl

She stood with a notepad and paper in hand.

It happens often after I have been speaking to a group of women: Someone wants to talk. This woman wanted something else. I knew it the minute I saw her stern and anxious look.

I had given a speech called "My Child Would Never." In this presentation, I talked about the freedom I gained from the realization that Luke and John were born with struggles, Sophie was born with an unusual ability, and I couldn't reproduce those characteristics if I tried. In realizing my identity as a daughter of God, instead of believing in my own abilities, I was able to love from a place of calm. I was able to parent from a place of grace. Trusting wholly in a Father, our perfect heavenly Father, who was a better parent than me. And yes, that meant letting my kids fall, so He could help them get back up.

The presentation had gone well. And as I made my way to the table the group had set up for me, the line was growing behind the woman with the pad and pen. She was dressed in a white shirt buttoned all the way to her neck and a floor-length denim skirt. Her white tennis shoes were scuff free. She wore no jewelry or makeup, and an enormous brunette bun streaked with gray was meticulously pinned on top of her head.

She stood glowering at me, disapproval in every line of her face. I towered over her in height, but I felt small in her presence as she looked me up and down and then said, "Well, that was a waste of my homeschool morning!"

"I'm sorry?" I inquired.

"I thought you were going to tell us how to stop our children from sinning! Instead, you are implying it is not my job to refine them with the rod so that they may become perfect as Christ is perfect."

I looked past her at the other moms, who appeared as shocked as I felt. A few even looked amused.

The woman raised her pen and pointed it at me. "I imagine you're just trying to sell books, so we have to wait to buy it to know what to do. Well, I want to know now. How do I stop my children from sneaking out windows? What do you recommend for a home alarm system? Did you take your son's phone? Was he using drugs? Do you have suggestions for punishments when they don't do their schoolwork?"

In the distance, I spied her children—no less than eight of them. All dressed in white button-downs and either denim skirts or khaki slacks. Her boys were getting restless, and she wanted answers.

I stood in silence.

"Well?" she barked. "What did you do to ruin your boy? Did you spare the rod? And are you local? Who is your daughter's piano teacher? Did she teach her how to play by ear?"

I was somewhere between tears and laughter. I felt like I could predict the future and see this woman's perfect control falling down around her. I silently prayed back my snark and cleared my throat. *Show me, Jesus. Show me what to say.*

"Oh, friend, I did all the things. We cannot stop our children from sinning. And their sin is not our sin. Love protects, but it also trusts. I see your children. It looks as though a couple of those strapping young men are about to be teenagers?"

She choked back tears and nodded. "My husband died last year in a roofing accident. I suffer from rheumatoid arthritis; some days, I can barely use my hands. I have to know how to control them. We have no internet, television, or cell phones. But I need to know, what else?" she begged. Her face was red, and beads of sweat collected on her brow.

I told her how sorry I was for her loss. And I said, "You are doing the things you feel will help. I didn't try those exact things with Luke, so I can't say if they would or would not have helped. And I am not local, but Sophie didn't start piano lessons until she was nine."

"You expect me to believe she can play like that video you showed without training? And I know there are answers! I know there are good kids who don't terrorize their families." The woman's voice fractured. "Just…never mind! As I suspected, this was a ploy to sell your book. I will be reading it, simply because I want to know what all the fuss is about, but I'll be checking it out at the library!"

Luckily, I didn't find the library jab humorous until the drive home. She stormed away, and I felt all the pangs of my past. All the stress of trying to keep myself in line and prevent my kids from sinning.

Let's consider that again.

Prevent my kids from sinning.

If I believed I could do that, what on earth was there for Jesus to do?

That night, I wrote out all the things I saw in the woman from that morning—traits I assumed she believed about herself:

Mother

Widow

Conservative

Organized

Modest

Detailed

Homeschooler

Believer

Law-follower

And I wished I could rewrite her list and start with *daughter*.

Daughter.

His girl.

Beloved.

Darling.

I had been where this woman stood. I had worked tirelessly to make God recognize me as special, but I didn't believe in my daughtership. And because I didn't believe in who God said I was, I was missing out on my inheritance. I thought there was always more for me to do.

I wanted to embrace this suffering sister and say to her, "The rules don't fix all the problems for all the children because none of the children are exactly the same. It's *you*. Your belief in Jesus is the thermostat for your home. If you believe you are a beloved daughter and your children are your siblings in Christ, God is the Father who will teach each of them…and you."

Perhaps the greatest lie of motherhood is that it somehow defines us as only *mother*, when in fact, we are wholly *daughter*. If we give birth, we become biological mothers, but that doesn't negate our birthright as daughters. And if we adopt? Still daughters. And if we are never mothers? Still, we are daughters.

Friend, what we are prior to our motherhood and long after is *daughters*. The care and keeping we afford these beings who call us "mom" define a part of our behaviors, but our identity is still fully in Christ.

Being a mother is fully consuming, and these humans we crave take every shred, every last morsel, and leave us with a rawness, an exposure that is pure bliss and equal terror. Still, let it be said, as much as I shed to them, I am fully consumed by the Father. Every prayer, hope, and last-ditch effort might be used by the enemy to distract me, to make me feel less—but still, there is my Father.

Gift-Bag Grace

One recent Christmas, I skipped the gift-bag monotony and opted to wrap the majority of our presents in thick, shiny, metallic paper. I secured enormous handmade bows, ornaments, and curly ribbons to each package. I had just as much fun preparing each gift as I did purchasing the treasures for what was an enormous brood of children. Eight, to be exact, with our foster daughter and Maggie's then-fiancé joining our traditional Christmas morning. We had an extended gift-giving marathon.

The collective laughter came each time one of the Vandals had their turn and were handed a gift box to open. For weeks, my little ones had begged to see what was inside each beautiful box. But did their little hands grab at bows and tear away paper? No. Each time, they brought their gift to me.

I didn't want to take over the fun of the task, so I would start by encouraging them.

"Tear the paper…"

"Pull off the bow…"

"Just rip into it…"

And each time, they looked utterly mystified.

Fair enough; Christmas is confusing. For the better part of a month, I had threatened them with, "Do not touch that!" and now I was basically insisting, "Destroy it." (Equally confusing: "Don't talk to strangers! But go sit in the fat man's lap and tell him all your hopes and dreams. I'll take your picture." Creepy.)

Given a gift bag with a wisp of tissue paper, the Vandals knew exactly what to do. It was easy. Straightforward. And, let's face it, a little boring.

As I watched their radically different responses to the two kinds of gift presentations, it hit me. This is how I have responded to the gift of grace. Jesus died so that I could walk in the freedom of redemption. Yet I have barely torn through the surface of the message. I may have tugged a corner to get a glimpse, pulled out a little tissue, even peeked a little inside, but I have not ravaged through to see the entirety of the treasure.

Early in my walk with God, I was handed the gift of grace in an easy-to-accept message: "Jesus died, and here is what you must do to complete the work." Like the Vandals, I know what to do with that. I have seen it my entire life. I remove the tissue and follow the rules. For years, I settled for gift-bag grace.

Certainly, I cannot just tear into the glorious gift of Jesus plus… nothing?

This is what I know: Follow the rules to complete the work of the cross.

That, my friends, is grace in chains.

Halfway into the gift giving, the Vandals finally became privy to the concept of wrapping paper and the joy of uncovering the treasures inside. They were anxious to help everyone else expose what was beneath the impressive packaging.

Grace unchained.

I wish I'd spent more time with the woman who threatened to read a library copy of my book. I wish I'd told her that grace is freedom from the law. That freedom doesn't lead us (or our children) into willful and chaotic sin binges. When we are in Christ, we have a desire to follow Him within us. That desire is what we need to cultivate in our children, because it's a desire that will outlast their childhoods and follow them all their lives.

If you believe you must do anything to perfect the work of the cross, grace is in chains. I have worked tirelessly to impress God, while He sees me as blameless. And when I stopped the façade and joined in the feast, I heard most clearly His voice, a voice that hums, "Mercy, my love." The voice of truth is a glorious song of freedom from works, joy in obedience.

Real Jesus Remains

When I fell into the arms of the Real Jesus and fell in love with the message of grace, there was a truth that helped me overcome anxiety about my children and their sin, their faith walk (or lack thereof), and their future. I poured these words of truth over my kids: "You walk in the favor of the Lord. He is with you, and He is for you. He died for you while you still sinned."

Sending semi-adult children off into the great beyond, I wonder...was it enough? Did I teach them everything they needed to know? I am not of the mind-set that the Jesus I love was wholly made theirs simply by my instruction. Scripture memory-work, "Jesus Loves Me," and Larry the Cucumber are a start, but God will have to take them to the finish line.

And what about these "temporary" sons and daughters of mine? There's a chance my foster children will hardly remember me, let alone recall the whispered prayers or the lullabies about a Jesus who adored them unto His death.

Bev Sheasby of Liberated Living Ministries poured these words into my heart: "Within the seed is the potential for the entire plant." If I planted an apple seed, I could water it; but would it be my work that would turn the seed into a tree? Would I be responsible for ensuring it produced a harvest? Could I accomplish this even if I wanted to? In Job 38, God asks, "Where were you when I laid the foundations of the earth?" (verse 4).

God gives the sunlight that feeds the sapling. He gives the water that nourishes it. He gives the nutrients from the earth below. He gives the wind that rustles the leaves. He does it all.

So I'll keep planting seeds and let my Father in heaven tend to them with loving care. He will nourish me, and He will do the same for my children. For your children.

If I could keep them from sinning, why would they need a Savior?

Chapter 17

SEEDS AND WEEDS

[Some] seeds fell among thorns that grew up
and choked out the tender plants. Still other
seeds fell on fertile soil, and they produced a
crop that was thirty, sixty, and even a hundred
times as much as had been planted!

MATTHEW 13:7-8

In parenting, there should be some kind of proverbial finish line one crosses. A point where you think, "Ah, at last. Here I rest." Spoiler alert: No.

Maggie is married and runs her own little online embroidery shop. John is a marine. Luke is living at home with us, working at a fair-trade company he adores while enrolled in college. Sophie is a sophomore in high school. Sam is in kindergarten, and Charlie is in preschool. Still, here I sit in the back of a police cruiser. I am being held for questioning for possession of narcotics. This is how I roll.

It was the day before Halloween. My first book, *Stolen Jesus,* had released earlier the same month. Luke and a friend borrowed my car. We exchanged words—he was late getting home, and I felt certain he had smoked in my car. A lingering odor met me when I climbed inside for a Walmart run to get a costume for Sam's literature parade at school the next morning.

I confess, I was stressed. The book launch had been mentally and emotionally draining. Justin was working out of town, and I was run ragged parenting alone. I made the conscious decision to indulge in a "treat."

I knew I shouldn't. I knew it was wrong. But I wanted what I wanted. Alone in my car, I opened the box and scarfed down three white powdered doughnuts before pulling out of the Walmart parking lot.

Then I cut loose and cried. I shoveled powdered comfort two-fisted into my mouth. With white powder mixed with salty tears caking on my face, I wailed and prayed. Apparently, I rolled through a stop sign.

The interior of my car became illuminated with red and blue light. I pulled over, reaching for a tissue and blowing my nose. The officer came to the passenger side of my car. I rolled down the window.

"Evening, ma'am. You realize you just rolled through that stop sign?"

"I'm so sorry, sir."

"Have you been crying?"

"Yes, it has been a long day."

He flashed his light to the back seat, illuminating the Vandals' car seats, then to the evidence of my doughnut binge, and then to the floorboard of the car. He looked at me and said, "Are these your drugs?"

I snort-laughed. My doughnuts? "I mean, I guess? I guess you could call them drugs."

"Ma'am, I need you to step out of the car and keep your hands visible."

"Okay?" I imagined my face covered in white powder. Did he think I was doing cocaine?

"Ma'am, I am putting you in my car. Anything you say or do in the car is being recorded."

"What do you mean?"

"I have reason to search the rest of your vehicle. While I am searching your vehicle, I need you to understand that anything you say or do in the police car is recorded and can be used against you."

"Can I text my kids? They'll be worried."

"Yes."

"You know, I was just kidding about the doughnuts. They aren't really drugs. I just sometimes need a little something to get me by."

"Ma'am, are you going to continue to pretend this is about doughnuts?"

He opened the back door of the police car. For the record, they really do put their hand on your head to guide you into the back seat.

"I am not pretending. I am really confused."

He looked at my license. "Mrs. Amerine, this detention is in regard to the bag of marijuana and pipe on the floorboard of your car. I am going to search the rest of your vehicle now." And he shut the door.

Know Who You Are

Among the prodigals and the perfected, the lost and the found, what is the goal of the parenting journey? My goal is that my children come to make Jesus Christ Lord of their hearts.

Not because it adds to my accolades. Not so I will somehow be applauded for raising them "right." But so that they might know the truth of who they are: noble.

If they are not hungry, how will they be fed?

If they are not thirsty, how will they long for living water?

If they are not tempted, how will they understand contentment?

If they are never lonely, outcast, or afraid, how will they recognize the lonely, outcast, and afraid among them?

If I prevent them from ever hurting, ever searching, or ever messing up, how will they ever know how much they need Jesus?

If I could keep them from sinning, why would they need a Savior?

I used to work myself in circles trying to make things easy for my kids. Cookies when they hurt, ice cream when they were broken. I have stood before coaches and begged for my kids to go first... to what end?

Did I, too, believe that these children's virginity, college degrees, parole records, or military rankings would count me more or less worthy of the cross? Do any of these things have the least effect on my identity as a daughter of God?

Do you know who you are?

Repeat after me:

> I am _____, of noble birth, daughter of the Most High. The children that I mother do not validate or negate my existence as God's daughter. I am adored. And I walk in the favor of the Lord, here on the sacred ground.

You Can Rest Here

Helicopter, free-range, homeschooling, public-schooling, conservative, liberal, widowed, divorced, lonely, skinny, fat, depressed, medicated, broken, or restored—we are mothers, and we are daughters. We may give birth into inflatable pools in the living room, use formula, or make placenta smoothies, but none of those choices define us. Christ in us does.

Our sons and daughters are uniquely fashioned, just as we are uniquely fashioned. We did not cease to exist when they came into creation, and their successes and failures do not make us any less or any more. Our worth as beloved daughters and our faith in Jesus

Christ cannot be contingent on whether our children graduate from college or go to prison. They might cure cancer; they may pass away before us. God remains, and we are still His.

For a moment, I wished I had known the name of the widow who confronted me at my presentation, so I could have addressed her by her name, but then I realized she is me, I am her, and we are of noble birth. She isn't right here, but two other women who need this message are: you and me.

Rest in this: God is a better parent than either of us. He parents you and me perfectly and will guide us through the trials, carrying us and our children over the hot coals, leaving us safely to rest and rejoice—here on the sacred ground.

Who Are You Again?

I sat, staring through a caged barrier at my little Toyota Crossover with the "Marine Mom" bumper sticker as police lights illuminated my neighborhood. The officer was kind enough to let me keep my phone. I texted Luke: "I AM GOING TO KILL YOU."

I texted Sophie: "Please call Daddy and tell him I am in police custody for possession of an illegal narcotic."

Sophie texted back: "Okay. Hey, do you know where my dance team bloomers are?"

I texted back: "In the laundry room in the red basket."

Luke texted: "What did I do?"

I texted back: "I am being held in the back of a police car for possession of an illegal narcotic."

Luke texted: "Mom??? Are you using?"

"I can't"…I deleted my first response.

I texted back: "No, son, I am not 'using.' But you left drugs in my car, and I got pulled over on a traffic violation, and now I am in the back of a police car."

Luke texted: "LOL, Mom, I don't have any drugs."

I texted back: "That's because you left them in my car."

I snapped a picture of my car being searched and sent it to him.

He texted back: "MOM! Don't say anything! If they try to arrest you, tell them they are my drugs."

I felt a twinge of pride. Not the kind of pride I felt when Maggie graduated from college or John became a marine, but that warm, fuzzy feeling when you realize one of your children would take one for the team.

The officer made his way back to the car and invited me to the front seat. There he produced some terribly tacky sunglasses, a stick of Bonne Bell lip gloss, a bag of marijuana, and a pipe. "Are these your items?" he asked.

I scoffed. "I would *never* wear those sunglasses."

He smiled and said, "I didn't think so."

At least he let me keep the doughnuts.

About 11:30 that night, I crawled into bed, my hair sopping wet and my room stuffy with shower steam and the scent of lavender. I heard the home alarm alert: "Garage. Door. Open."

That lanky walk and his striking features still slay me. This boy-man, Luke Henry.

"Heeey, hey! Shawshank!"

I know, but I laughed. "Luke, son… I can't."

He flopped on the bed and we laughed, harder than I have laughed maybe ever.

Who am I?

I am mother to a brood of talents, patriots, criminals, artists, temporary, permanent, young, old…humans.

Who am I?

Writer, wife, author, artist, binge eater, comedian, drama queen, friend, enemy, boss, employee…criminal.

Who am I?

I am a daughter, afforded amazing grace. Adored. Cherished. Forgiven.

And in that instant, with a hippie man-baby sprawled on my bed, I wasn't mad. I wasn't worried or afraid. I was desperately in love and eternally hopeful about this child, this boy who tested my limits and drove me to doughnuts.

Son.

Daughter.

Children.

One Father, who totally gets us.

Here on the sacred ground.

Epilogue

HERE I AM

I heard the Lord asking, "Whom should I send
as a messenger to this people? Who will go
for us?" I said, "Here I am. Send me."

ISAIAH 6:8

On this day, I am writing to you a word about parenting. To parent, and to be parented.

On this day, John started a 54-hour challenge known as the Crucible. This endurance test, the capstone to his recruit training, is what he has to accomplish to be a marine. Forty-five miles of striving over hills and through rough terrain, and days of food and sleep deprivation. My heart held anxiety and dread and many prayers as I read and reread the letter my son sent to me before he left for this challenge.

> You won't hear from me again from boot camp. By the time you get this, I will be on the Crucible, and then you'll be here for graduation. I only get two MREs [meals ready to eat] for the entire three days. Sometimes there are Skittles…I hope I get Skittles. Hey, please bring me my cowboy boots. I miss my boots. Love, John

Jesus, please Lord Jesus, give my baby Skittles.

For a moment, this was my most ardent prayer, and then I heard her.

"Hi! Mommy! Mommy! Hi! Mommy!"

Her bare feet pitter-pattered across the hardwood floor of my office. Her tiny blonde pigtails were lopsided on her sleep-scented head. She was warm from her nap. The fragrance—let me coin it, lest I ever forget: Pampers, Desitin, urine, lavender-scented Johnson & Johnson baby shampoo, Cheerios, and sunshine.

I knew the hill I had to climb. At nearly the same hour that we hoped to receive the news about our boy completing the Crucible and becoming a marine, a car was going to pull out from our driveway. In it would be this baby girl whom I had fostered and mothered for nearly two years. She was going be delivered from our lives and into her birth mother's arms forever. My heart rejoiced with this restoration, but I can't pretend my heart wasn't simultaneously breaking. None of this was easy.

Recruit mom to marine mom.

"Mommy" to just some lady she won't remember.

Jesus, please Lord Jesus, let me never forget.

7\\95830j cxzkcccm///;oikhhhhhnnnnnnn/z. Her little fingers typed on the page. Please, dear editor, just leave this reminder. Her tiny fingers were here. Her body was in my arms.

This Is Motherhood

In one day, I had all the emotions. Some don't even have names, there were so many. There were other needs in my family, but in that moment, my heart was heavy for my almost-marine and the sweet girl I had to release.

This is motherhood.

In a matter of seconds, my prayers shifted from pleas for Skittles to deep mama-soul laments and requests for intervention and protection for my kids.

This is motherhood too: Holding the ordinary and the holy in our clasped, ready-for-prayer hands with a grip so tight, we wonder how we can ever let go.

Thankless? Yes.

A treacherous hike, definitely.

Food and sleep deprivation.

No promise of the outcome.

Moms don't have to run the Crucible; we live out the ultimate endurance challenge. And it lasts a lot longer than 54 hours.

We Are Called Here

I propose that motherhood is the closest we come to understanding how methodically God loves us. That is why we are called here to this place. This is the place where we hand over our hearts and our children to a God who loves them more than we can fathom. This is what it looks like to give your whole heart, be utterly disappointed and defeated, sticky, smelly, exhausted, worried, broken, in police custody, and completely and unmistakably in love.

And loved.

In more than twenty years of parenting, I have learned much, but the most important lesson is that God can make our messes sacred. Faith in God's existence is one thing; believing Him is another. My exhausting efforts—far from perfect, yet genuine in intention—shy in comparison to who He is and the glory He brings to my messes.

From the first time we were called "Mom," our identities were forever changed. So, too, we were transformed the moment we said *yes* to Christ. We are forever His daughters. We are forever perfected by the work of the cross. Believing *in* God isn't the key to peace and happiness; believing God is. Peace can be ours—peace in spite of difficulties—when we do life with God. This is the peace that will sustain us.

God calls us to be here. Right here. On common ground and the sacred ground of our homes—sticky floors and all. And together we reply to the Lord, "Here I am."

Last night a precious, wounded little girl arrived at our home.

We just said goodbye to the little girl we'd loved for two years—the girl who called me "Mommy." After that experience, we seriously considered pulling our foster license and discontinuing our involvement in the program. No matter how worthy the work, the grieving process for that removal is foot-of-the-cross work. I lie there often and grieve in the arms of a Father who knows Joy-Baby and loves her more than I can fathom.

But we got the call, and I told our agency I would call Justin and run it by him.

Me: "We have a placement request."

Justin: "No."

Me: "Okay."

Justin: "Wait…what's up?"

Me: "She's 26 months old, injured, already in a cast. Hispanic, not from our area. They can transport her."

Justin: "Long term or short?"

Me: "Long."

Justin: "Any issues?"

Me: "Well, she's injured, but no sexual abuse reported. The caseworker says she's independent, cuddly, and she sings…like Disney movie songs."

Justin: "Ugh. Aren't we boycotting Disney?"

Me: "Not since 2001."

Justin: "Is she adoptable?"

Me: "Seriously?"

Justin: "I know, I know. I just wish sometimes we knew for sure. What's her name?"

Me: "Melody."

Justin: "Why can't they ever offer us a Larry or an Archibald with a bad attitude?"

Me: "I don't know. Should I ask for an awful baby?"

Justin: "No, don't."

Me: "So, no?"

Justin: "No…no, tell them we will do it."

Me: "Oh."

Justin: "I know."

Me: "We have problems."

Justin: "Yep…"

AFTERWORD

My name is Luke Henry Amerine. I am agnostic, but I cling to the idea that there is a God who loves me. I wear Birkenstocks when I plow the wheat fields for my dad. I am a pescatarian, but sometimes all I want is a steak. I hate the idea of putting God in a box; I put God in a box every day.

I am not one thing—no one is one thing or one way. Everyone is on a journey, and the farther along we go, the more paradoxical the journey becomes. To say that a man is one way is to say that he isn't another. We are what we think we are, not what others label us.

This is hard for us to grasp, for we are bound to our physicality, and we are inclined to labels and looks. We love planning; we love an answer, a reason. In my search for a God who loves me, I have come to understand that we are free from the labels that bind us and hold us down. We are far greater than our flesh. I'd like to think of my life as a beginning rather than a finished story—an ever-changing and ever-growing thing that cannot fit in a box.

To have been asked to write this was a great honor. I am of noble birth, and I am loved well in all the stickiness, raised here on the sacred ground.

More from Jami Amerine

Now that you've finished reading *Sacred Ground, Sticky Floors,* please enjoy the first chapter of *Stolen Jesus,* Jami's journey to discover the real Jesus.

Stealing Jesus

Thus says the LORD who made the earth,
the LORD who formed it to establish it—
the LORD is his name: Call to me and I will
answer you, and will tell you great and
hidden things that you have not known.

JEREMIAH 33:2-3 ESV

I am a walking contradiction. Let's establish this from the start.

I am a lover of Jesus and abundant joy. I am a wife and mother of six, maybe seven or eight. A homeschooler and PTA mom. An aerobics instructor and binge eater. A marathon runner this week; a champion puff-pastry artist the next. I have a type A personality with type C tendencies. I'm a vegan on Monday, and an "I'll take my steak rare!" lunatic by Friday. I am a cattle ranch owner who loves city living. I'm a blacklisted Mormon and a displaced Catholic attending an instrumental Church of Christ. (That means lots of toe tapping and banjo strumming.)

I worship at the feet of a genie-in-a-bottle Jesus when the line at Starbucks gets too long and I am going to be late to Pilates. And

I bawl like a baby when we have to turn away a foster placement, unable to help a child in need. I have a degree in home economics, but I can't thread a needle. I can make yeast rolls that would drive you to weep. I am allergic to wheat.

I want the warm, cozy feelings I experience in my prayer chair to last forever, but I am tightly wound. I am a worrier. And I am terrified of many things—vomit, flying, roller coasters, crunchy bugs, and egg salad primarily.

My mortal claim to fame is that even though I've had no training, I can play the drums like Phil Collins, and I can rap perfectly in sync to the Beastie Boys, *all of their songs*. And I can do that without missing a lick after a worship singalong with Francesca Battistelli. The weight of this paradox is not lost on me.

I seem to fail at many things. And when I don't fail, I get so bolstered with pride, it is sinful. My entire existence is a study in contradictions.

And yet I tread on the sacred. My reality doesn't change who Jesus is. I propose we are so used to making Him fit our world and our brains that we have missed out on experiencing the richness of Him. Our society, busy minds, bad theology, and first-world living have robbed us of a priceless commodity. And what's been taken from us? Jesus. The *real* Jesus.

So here I am. An almost high school dropout with a master's degree. A dyslexic author. A foot racer with bad knees and broken arches. I am filling out college scholarship applications for two children and preschool submissions for another while bouncing a newborn in a sling (and did I mention I don't have a uterus?). I am certified to teach eleven different aerobics classes, but I need to lose sixty pounds. I crave honesty and a rawness I don't always find in the church pew, yet I try to never miss a Sunday. And I believe in being nice, and obeying the law—and still, I stole Jesus.

My first image of Jesus came from the Mormon church. *Head of Christ*, the famous painting by Warner Sallman, hung in every ward (the neighborhood church) and also in the Mormon temple. This is still the image I see whenever I hear the name of Jesus. Over the years, long after I left the Mormon church, I would occasionally see this familiar painting of what I thought of as "Mormon Jesus," and I felt as if I were seeing an old friend.

Then, in 2005, I began to teach aerobics classes at a local YMCA. I was delighted the first time I walked into the lobby and was greeted by the painting. One afternoon, after I taught a cycling class, I was clocking out when I noticed that the portrait of Jesus was gone. It had been replaced with a dry-erase board.

Confused—because the joint is a Christian organization and the sweet face of our Christ was constantly in view—I asked the receptionist, "Where's Jesus?"

"Oh! He's behind the filing cabinet." She pointed toward the back of the office. "Management thinks He's too old-fashioned."

So, sneaking Him out unseen, I took Stolen Jesus home with me.

Now He hangs over the mantel, a fugitive from the YMCA, and we are proud to have Him there. On many occasions, I have sat in our living room and talked to Stolen Jesus, the Jesus I made my own when He was rejected. With His rock-star mullet, dreamy blue eyes, and olive complexion, He is calm and constant. He never seems bothered or troubled.

His familiar presence changes things. Once my husband and I got into an argument in the living room, and we quickly remembered Stolen Jesus was watching. I said, "We really shouldn't yell in front of Stolen Jesus..." So, we moved to the kitchen and forgot what we were arguing about. Sometimes we catch ourselves: "Don't say that in front of Stolen Jesus!" Or I'll chirp to one of our toddlers, Sam and Charlie, whom we lovingly call the Vandals, "Really? You're naked in front of Stolen Jesus?" And I know Jesus is much more than a moral compass, much more than a painting. But to have Him in our living room is a reminder of who we should be...who I wish I was.

As much as I have grown to know and love that image, it wasn't until we began our journey in foster care that I realized I didn't know Jesus as well as I thought I did. It occurred to me that I had given Him characteristics based on human interactions. I had waited for others to explain Him to me. Worse still, I had allowed Him to be stolen *from me.* And it was at the end of one terrible day that I came to the realization I needed to get to know Him on my own.

———

The morning started out poorly. My husband, Justin, and I don't argue a lot, but on this certain morning we'd gotten into a full-blown battle about disciplining one of the kids. Justin had taken away our middle son Luke's phone. While I was in agreement about the need for training, the loss of that particular phone really punished *me.* This child would almost certainly nag me to death until his phone was returned to him. Moreover, I would be unable to reach him on a day he had two appointments. Without his phone, I would have to unload babies from their car seats and venture up several flights of stairs in two different locations to retrieve him. Of course, I could make other provisions for him, but at the moment the phone was confiscated, I was dismayed.

Sophie, who was twelve at the time, was cranky over some missing papers, and when Sophie gets cranky, *just stand back*. (I cannot imagine where she gets the drama gene.) John and his brother Luke, both in their early teens, were bickering in the kitchen over the last piece of bacon, and both Sam, a toddler, and our foster son had been up and down several times during the night. (We hadn't adopted Charlie yet, but if he'd been in the picture, he would have been a mess too.) As I was getting everyone into the car, Justin barked, "Are you taking the baby to the doctor so we can get some sleep?"

I yawned back at him and said, "No. I don't have time today, and I think he's just teething."

Justin barked, "Well, *perfect*! I forgot he has to get teeth!"

I glared at him while he stormed past me, slamming the door. I sighed heavily. I was forty-three years old, with a borrowed newborn, and honestly, teething had slipped my mind too...that and potty training. But I wasn't about to let Justin know that.

I drove the kids to school. I looked a fright. I hadn't gotten up before the children, and I was still wearing my pajamas. I hadn't put on a bra, and my dirty Ugg boots adorned my already tired feet. We pulled up to the school, and John asked, "Can you come inside to sign my permission slip?"

I am not a woman who can go without a bra, so I explained to my son that I would *not* be going into the office. This vexed John, apparently more than having his braless, pajama-clad mother inside his school, but he grouchily agreed to bring the permission slip out to me. The wait in the office for the slip caused him to be tardy, which did nothing to improve anyone's mood.

As I drove the babies home, I couldn't stop yawning, fantasizing about the huge cup of coffee I'd enjoy while the babies played and I dozed in my prayer chair with Stolen Jesus.

Coffee. Coffee. Coffee. And then...

And then I remembered: I hadn't gone to the store the day before. We were out of coffee.

We were out of coffee.

Trying not to cry, I hopped on the drive-thru loop for Starbucks. I pulled up in line behind forty cars. Thirty minutes later I ordered *two* venti coffees, which would enable me to guzzle coffee until noon. Mustering a smile, I advanced to the window to pay. To my horror, I realized I didn't have my wallet. And I started to cry.

The barista took pity on what was clearly a desperate situation and said, "Uh, it's okay, ma'am. This one's on the house!" Weeping with gratitude and humiliation, but with coffee in hand, I vowed that I'd be back that afternoon to pay for my order. I cried and drove, talking out loud to myself or Americanized Jesus about my first-world problems. As I turned onto my street, I noticed a blue car sitting in front of our house. *Who in the world is that?* I drove past the car to pull into the garage and realized it was the foster baby's caseworker from Child Welfare.

Surprise inspection.

"You have got to be *kidding* me!" I said out loud, this time directly to Jesus.

I closed the garage and got Sam and the baby out of their car seats. They were both still in their jammies, and both looked a little...*crusty*. But there was no time for a bra or a change of clothes; the caseworker was already ringing the doorbell.

I begrudgingly let her into the house, apologizing for being such a mess. I explained that we'd had a rough night and a harsh morning while she wrote something down on her yellow notepad. *Really?* I offered her a seat in the living room, casting a cold stare at Stolen Jesus and mouthing the words, "Dude, help!" I spread a blanket on the floor for the baby and sat next to him. Sam talked gibberish to the caseworker for a minute, and I told him to please go watch Elmo.

Notepad in hand, the caseworker started in on about a thousand questions to which I responded while playing with the baby. At about the moment I thought the whole experience could not get any worse, Sam came in carrying a glass jar of pickles from Costco, about the same size as Sam himself. He also held a fork, a knife, a spoon, and, because he is not an animal, a napkin. He came to a stop directly over the baby, whose cranium was in full jeopardy of being squashed by the fifteen-pound jar of pickles.

The caseworker leaped out of her chair and snatched up the blameless babe just as the huge jar slipped to the ground where baby's head had been. Without missing a lick, I joked, "Nice save!"

Innocently, Sam said, "Mommy, bweakfas?" The look on the caseworker's face shifted from horror to disbelief as I pried open the jar of pickles and began feeding them to Sam, picnic-style, on the floor in the formal living room. But her incredulity was wasted on me. Surely this could not have been the worst environment she would see that day?

Taking the baby back from the caseworker, I answered her questions about our evacuation plans in the event of fire, nuclear war, or civil unrest. (Yes, this is for real.) She collected her notepad and stood up, asking to see the baby's bed and our fire extinguishers. Carrying Baby, I led her back to our room to show her the baby's crib, which was when I spotted them:

Rolaids.

They were on Justin's nightstand; she saw them too. She gasped. I'm not even exaggerating: The woman *gasped*. "Oh dear!" she said. "I'm going to have to write you up for this infraction. When I get back to the office, I will notify my supervisor about the unsecured medications. We'll have to meet to discuss it with licensing."

Being written up for the near death-by-pickles, I would have understood, but *Rolaids?* That was my last straw for the day, and it was only nine o'clock, which is pretty early for the last straw.

Feeling both exasperated and feisty, I pounced. "I'm sure my husband just forgot to put them up, and this baby can't walk or crawl. And it's not narcotics—it's *antacid*."

She looked at me forebodingly, again scratching rebuke on her little yellow notepad. "Medications must be kept out of children's reach."

"Well, *technically*, since he cannot stand, it *is* out of his reach. And it's not like I was cooking meth!"

She considered me over her eyeglasses with condescension worthy of a librarian and continued writing.

Now I was the one who categorically needed some Rolaids, and I wanted my coffee. She finally left, and I knew I would be hearing from our caseworker any minute. I went to get the cold Starbucks from the car to nuke it. Plopping down in my prayer chair, I glared at Stolen Jesus, and I made this vow out loud: "If they pull our foster license and come get this baby, I am going to insist that they take the other children too—biological and adopted. And then I am getting back in bed and eating pickles and taking a nap."

Stolen Jesus didn't respond.

It wasn't long before the phone rang, and I had to explain the Rolaids thing. I ate pickles for lunch, and I didn't get a nap. I drudged through the rest of the day, loading up the babies and going to Starbucks to pay for the morning's coffee and to get a third venti to go. I ran my older son to his appointments without incident (despite his lack of a cell phone), grabbed some pizzas, and came home. By seven o'clock, the baby was in bed and so was I. Justin helped the others with homework, and at some point, we apologized to each other for our viciousness earlier in the day.

I felt like a loser. Later that night, unable to sleep, I got up and went to the kitchen. I grabbed some gluten-free, low-fat cookies and Reese's Peanut Butter Cups and headed to sit with Stolen Jesus.

I flipped open my Bible, but I didn't have the energy to search out any wisdom. I didn't have the strength to process anything. I certainly did not need a lesson in who begat whom. I just needed a single word to drown out the voices in my head as I listed my failures. A voice whispered, "He won't want to say anything to you after your awful day." And I agreed with that voice. And then my eyes landed on Matthew 5:3:

Blessed are the poor in spirit...

Chills ran up my spine. I looked up at Stolen Jesus. Everyone was asleep, and they'd seen me talk to Him on many occasions, but still, I whispered, "Is that for me?"

He didn't say anything.

"This was all a punishment, wasn't it?"

Blessed are the poor in spirit...

A lump rose in my throat. "I don't know You at all, do I? I have all of these voices in my head and characteristics I believe about You, but I don't know what's real. This ghastly condemnation I feel—is this from You? Mormon Jesus wouldn't want me to be obsessed with coffee...but You? Real Jesus? Do You rebuke people for drinking coffee? Are You mad about the Rolaids? Are You mad because I deliver kids to school in my pajamas? Are You just mad?"

Blessed are the poor in spirit...

I sat in silence, and in that moment I was relieved to admit I was falling behind. I *was* poor in spirit, but in my poverty He was calling me blessed.

It occurred to me that I'd believed in (and broken up with) a lot of Jesuses over the years, but never a Jesus who had called me blessed. I'd believed in a Mormon Jesus, and a High School Jesus, and Justin's Jesus...but never, I think, the Real Jesus. My heart was racing.

I was swamped with a deep need to start over, to go back to the first time I heard His name. I wanted to relearn Jesus at the lowest level of understanding. Baby talk. Small words. A simple unfolding. An evolution, getting to know Him based on what I was developmentally capable of understanding, not trying to grasp Him from a lofty theological view.

I confess that I'd often thought of spirituality as a race, with everyone else running faster and farther ahead of me. But I realized that I didn't need to rush to keep up. I could back up, slow down. Falling behind had to be better than faking belief. I wouldn't ask a new bride to speed ahead fifteen years. Take your time, burn dinner, fight over the checkbook, and watch movies holding hands.

Discover each other.

For years I had professed an adoration for Jesus Christ, but in my poor state, on that night, I knew it was more habit than a relationship, more culture than worship, more clan than companionship. And I was undone. I wanted to have a real come-to-Jesus. I wanted the experience to be as genuine as possible.

It was time for a whole new Jesus.

Real Jesus.

I promise I could feel Him in the room. My mind raced, and I begged the feeling to stay. I wished I could be someone else, someone who was able to be fully present all the time. Someone whose mind never wandered to grocery lists during the sermon, someone whose Bible reading was never interrupted with shrieks. I wanted the depth of that moment to last forever.

And then I heard our foster son begin to cry, and I cried too.

Blessed are the poor in spirit.

Fine, I decided. I couldn't exist in a hypnotic state of bliss and remain euphorically high on Jesus. I rushed to tend to the baby and rushed back to the chair and willed my mind back to the idyllic state I had experienced moments before the hollers.

I reached in my Bible study bag and pulled out a journal and pen, and I asked Real Jesus to show Himself to me. Words poured from the pen. Pleas emptied from my heart. Once the ball started rolling, there was no stopping the process. So much of what I embraced about Jesus had been formulated decades ago. Fear, shame, and legalism were definitely issues I needed to deal with. Out loud I said, "Search my heart. Help me start over! Help me escape the lies and the torture of letting You down every single day." My pen flew across the pages of the journal: "Bad things happen, good things happen, and He stays. *He is always here.*"

I wept and wrote. I confessed and begged. And sometime after three in the morning, I came to a place where I knew that as complex as I am, as diverse as my children are, so must be the One who fashioned us. He knows the flaws and inconsistencies that make me all Jami, all the time. From my lofty marathon goals to my adoration for Sunday naps and homemade pie, He is able to hold all my contradictions and weave them into one beautiful whole. The journey of discovery was just beginning.

I was startled from the reverie when Justin stumbled down the hall and said, "Geez, Jami, who in the world are you talking to in the middle of the night?"

Without hesitation, I blurted, "Just Jesus."

NOTES

Part 1

1. Gerald L. Sittser, *The Will of God as a Way of Life* (Grand Rapids, MI: Zondervan, 2000), 32.

Chapter 2

1. Jami Amerine, "Go, and Don't Believe Everything I Taught You..." *Sacred Ground, Sticky Floors*, January 12, 2016, http://sacredgroundstickyfloors.com/2016/01/12/go-and-dont-believe-everything-i-taught-you/.

Chapter 13

1. Christy Mobley, "The Last of First Goodbyes," *Joying in the Journey* (blog), August 2, 2016, http://christymobley.com/2016/08/02/the-last-of-first-goodbyes/.

Chapter 15

1. Elizabeth Smart, quoted by Molly Oswaks, "Elizabeth Smart Is Standing Up for Rape Victims—And Tearing Down Purity Culture," *Broadly*, September 1, 2016, https://broadly.vice.com/en_us/article/elizabeth-smart-is-standing-up-for-rape-victimsand-tearing-down-purity-culture.

Acknowledgments

To you my Lord Jesus, had I known the road You would lead me down I might have changed out of my pajamas, dressed nicer, run a brush through my hair, cried and cursed less. Thank You for loving me so dearly despite that folly. All glory and honor are Yours forever my Love.

Special thanks to my family.

Justin, I like-like you. Thank you for picking me for this journey. You are wonderful.

Maggie, Christian, John, Luke, Sophie, Sam, Charlie, and our little foster-love—forever you are breath, story, and inspiration. I adore you each.

Thank you, Daddy. Truly you granted me the vision of the depths of Fatherly love. I am able to believe in my birthright because of how well you love me as daughter. You are an imprint on my soul of selfless and lifegiving love.

Mom, you are my friend. I am only able to write these things because of the writer who raised me.

Stacey and Dean, Michael and Kelly, and the Pixies and Vandals thank you for your prayers and support. You are most dear to me.

To my friends and sisters Kim Phelan, Marcy Toppert, Lisa Carroll, Lisa Williamson, Bobbi Pledger, Holly Blackwell, Shawna Mathis, Wynema Clark, Trisha Gunn, Jeane Wynn, Anna LeBaron, Shelby Spear, Katie Reid, Carey Scott, Rebecca Huff—your prayers, friendship, and wisdom have made me better, dried my tears, strengthened my faith, and created the person I am today.

To Katie and Adam Reid your hammock/fireside chats and encourage-ment bring a smile to my face and vibrant thoughts to my wild mind. I am ever grateful to have you in my life. Thank you for all the extra reading and your unfailing support. Katie, you are the dog's meow.

Rebecca Huff you have blessed and challenged me in great ways. Thank you for being my friend.

Lorraine Reep since the beginning…I love you.

Christy Mobley I treasure your wisdom and words.

Carey Scott, where have you been all my life? To my unruly band of wordsmith sisters, my Build a Sister Up tribe, as well as, Jaclyn Harwell, Tracy Levinson, Christine Carter, Kate Battestelli, Jenny Rapson, and Jan Greenwood and all of Jessie's Girls, I love you guys.

To Mary Allen, I penned this book as I have watched from afar as you have mothered well, grieved beautifully, and truly walked out motherhood and a love of Jesus in fine form. Thank you. Someday I hope you know how much I admire you and the way you mother. Rage on.

To my Facebook friends and Hopelively gang—you are truly my tribe. Thank you hardly does justice.

To John and Beverly Sheasby, your words and ministry change lives, I will forever hear my God with a South African accent. I love you both.

To Christian Homes and Family Services, you completed us. May your work and mission continue to provide hope and joy in the lives of many.

Special thanks to John Vonhoff, Kathy Ide, Judy Morrow, Marci Seither, Kathi Lipp, and all the beautiful people at Mount Hermon Christian Writers Conference.

For Jessica Kirkland, my friend and agent. You are the best.

Kathleen Kerr, my friend and editor, you have the patience of Job. I am glad you are still sane after this book baby, truly I know it was a mess of momma emotions only another mother could decipher.

To Bob, Sherrie, Jessica, Christianne, Betty, and all the beautiful crew at Harvest House Publishers—thank you for believing in me, trusting me, and letting me say all the things. I am privileged to call you "my house." This is home.

About the Author

Jami Amerine is the author of *Stolen Jesus* and the creator of the popular blog *Sacred Ground, Sticky Floors*, where she posts about Jesus, parenting, marriage, and the general chaos of life. She holds a master's degree in Education, Counseling, and Human Development. Jami and her husband, Justin, have six kids and are active in foster care.

To learn more about Jami Amerine or to read sample chapters, visit our website at www.harvesthousepublishers.com

To learn more about Harvest House books and
to read sample chapters, visit our website:

www.harvesthousepublishers.com

HARVEST HOUSE PUBLISHERS
EUGENE, OREGON